All rights reserved. No part of this publication may be reproduced, distributed, or transmitted in any form or by any means, including photocopying, recording, or other electronic or mechanical methods, without prior written permission of the Author.

Table of Contents

A word from the Author 7
Introduction 11
Erotism or Eroticism in Management? 15
The Power of Seduction in Management 23
The Seductive Communication 67
The Art of Persuasion 135
Developing Charisma 166
Leadership and Sensuality 200
Talent Management from a Sensual Perspective 229
Success, Power, and Attraction 273
Unleashing the Power: Erotism as an Unexplored Business Resource 299
So, what is SENSUAL INTELLIGENCE? 309
Afterword from the Author: The Power to Transform 328

A word from the Author

Welcome to a brave exploration of an unchartered territory in the world of business management. Allow me to present "*Seducing Success: Mastering Sensual Intelligence in Business*" an audacious perspective on leadership, urging you to challenge the established conventions, and venture into a captivating world of erotism in management.

This is not a book that sanctions uncontrolled sexualization or unethical manipulation. Instead, it examines the deeper layers of human connection and emotion, proposing an enthralling concept: What if the secrets to powerful leadership lay in the alluring realm of erotism, an underappreciated yet potent force?

Erotism, in its myriad forms, has been an enigmatic force guiding human interactions and relationships throughout history. Strikingly, its potential in the business world has often been overlooked, even outright dismissed. This book aims to upturn such dismissals and unfurl the rich tapestry of leadership potential woven in the threads of erotic energy.

In its core, erotism surpasses the mere physical or sexual. It thrives on the pulsating exchange of energy and passion, the magnetism that binds individuals together, and the creation of an environment that breeds trust, collaboration, and motivation.

"Seducing Success" promises an immersive journey, taking you from understanding erotism's crucial role in the business landscape, through the exploration of its role in enhancing leadership and creativity, to the mastery of seductive communication and ethical persuasion tactics.

With this book as your guide, you will uncover how to master the art of seductive body language, manipulate voice and tone effectively, and leverage nonverbal communication to make a lasting impact on your team. In tandem, you will learn to wield the sword of persuasion with respect and integrity, inspiring others to realize their true potential and work towards shared goals.

This exploration extends to a deep dive into personal charisma, understanding and honing your unique traits that cultivate an emotional connection with your team. By balancing this personal magnetism with efficient leadership, you can create a work dynamic that is mutually beneficial, inspiring, and committed.

Leadership and sensuality are closely interlinked, with desire and attraction serving as potent sources of motivation and inspiration. This book will guide you on creating a stimulating work environment that boosts performance, catalyzes growth, and encourages the development of individuals and teams alike.

"Seducing Success" also takes a sensual approach to talent management, teaching you how to attract and retain top professionals, and use erotic elements appropriately to foster their professional development.

Lastly, we delve into the intricate relationship between success, power, and attraction. Striking a balance between these forces is vital to fostering a productive dynamic in the business environment.

As the journey through this book concludes, it will leave you with practical applications of these concepts, ready to be implemented in your professional life. This book is a testament to challenging stereotypes and overcoming prejudices to unlock new paths to success.

"Seducing Success: Mastering sensual Intelligence in Business" is an open invitation to shed old paradigms, embrace novel ideas, and embark on a transformative journey in leadership and management. Join us on this exploration, and let's together redefine the boundaries of success.

Antonio Garrido

Introduction

In the dynamic landscape of business, management is a vibrant field, ripe for the discovery of groundbreaking strategies that spearhead growth and success. As leaders, we navigate a labyrinth of daily challenges, from directing teams to making critical decisions, with our eyes fixed on achieving extraordinary results. Amid the well-trodden paths of traditional approaches and established theories, there lies an intriguing, largely untouched territory: erotism. However, we elevate this exploration by introducing a more encompassing concept: sensual intelligence.

Welcome to "*Seducing Success: Mastering Sensual Intelligence in Business.*" This audacious and transformative book beckons you to traverse the uncharted terrains of leadership and business management. We invite you to challenge preconceived norms and discover how the power of seduction, underpinned by sensual intelligence, can be your secret weapon in magnifying influence and reaching new pinnacles of success in the corporate world.

Erotism, teeming with sensuality and magnetism, has held humanity in its thrall since antiquity. Yet, its relevance in the business environment has often been dismissed or completely ignored. This book turns this narrative on its head, revealing how erotism, when applied mindfully, can not only coexist with management but elevate it to unforeseen heights.

The book offers an in-depth examination of erotism in management, unpacking its essential components and presenting practical strategies to infuse it into your leadership repertoire. This exploration doesn't advocate for unchecked sexualization or irresponsible manipulation; instead, it centers on comprehending and harnessing the enticing force of erotism to foster authentic connections, inspire trust, and amplify team performance.

Here, erotism in management extends beyond the mere physical or sexual implications. It's about engaging with the energy and passion coursing between individuals, understanding the allure of emotional attraction, and constructing a work environment that bolsters trust, collaboration, and motivation.

In our journey through the pages of "*Seducing Success: Mastering Sensual Intelligence in Business,*" we'll scrutinize various facets of erotism in the corporate setting, breaking taboos and discarding stereotypes linked with its use. We'll delve into how erotic energy can powerfully enhance leadership, stimulate creativity, and catalyze innovation.

In the sphere of communication, you'll unravel how seductive body language, and the strategic use of voice and tone can significantly impact how your team perceives and connects with you. We'll delve into the criticality of nonverbal communication and its effective deployment in conveying messages, leaving an indelible impact on your team.

Persuasion, another crucial element of sensual intelligence, will be examined, and we'll explore strategies based on attraction, learning to fashion an appealing environment for employees while establishing ethical parameters to deter manipulation. This ethical, impactful persuasion can ignite others' passion and help realize organizational goals.

As we venture into the realm of charisma, you'll learn to identify and amplify your charismatic traits, cultivating empathy, and emotional connections with your team. This personal magnetism, coupled with efficacious leadership, can catalyze a work dynamic that elevates motivation and commitment.

Additionally, we'll probe the relationship between leadership and sensuality, unraveling how desire and attraction can serve as potent sources of inspiration. From the lens of talent management, we'll discuss how to attract and retain the cream of the crop through a sensual approach, effectively utilizing erotic elements to boost their professional growth.

In conclusion, "*Seducing Success: Mastering Sensual Intelligence in Business*" emboldens you to broaden your perspectives and embrace a transformative approach to leadership and management. By challenging stereotypes and overcoming biases, this book illuminates a path to unearthing new growth opportunities and catapulting your career to unprecedented success.

Erotism or Eroticism in Management?

Erotism or eroticism in the context of business management is an intriguing concept that explores the use of sensual qualities and emotions to create a more profound and engaging work environment. While the terms erotism and eroticism may seem similar, they have distinct applications and implications in the field of management.

Erotism in business management goes beyond the traditional understanding of sexuality and sexual desire. It does not promote inappropriate or explicit interactions in the workplace. Instead, it emphasizes the recognition and validation of human emotions, passions, and desires within a professional setting. It seeks to create an atmosphere where individuals can freely express their passions and desires in a respectful and professional manner.

The concept of erotism in management acknowledges the diverse range of emotions that humans experience and understands that these emotions can significantly impact the workplace. By embracing and addressing these emotions, managers can cultivate a more holistic and fulfilling work experience for their employees. This approach recognizes that individuals are not just rational beings driven solely by logic but also emotional beings with desires, dreams, and aspirations.

One of the primary goals of incorporating erotism in business management is to foster deeper connections among team members. By recognizing and appreciating the emotional aspects of individuals, managers can create an environment that encourages open communication, empathy, and collaboration. When employees feel understood and supported, they are more likely to engage with their work on a deeper level, leading to increased creativity, productivity, and job satisfaction.

Furthermore, erotism in management acknowledges that employees are not mere cogs in a machine but unique individuals with their own aspirations and desires. This approach encourages managers to tap into the intrinsic motivations of their employees and align their work tasks with their personal passions and interests. By doing so, managers can create a work environment that sparks enthusiasm and fosters a sense of fulfillment, ultimately leading to higher levels of employee engagement and performance.

However, it is important to differentiate erotism from eroticism in business management. Eroticism in management involves a focus on explicit sexual content, desire, or arousal within the workplace. Introducing such explicit sexual elements into a professional setting can be highly inappropriate and potentially lead to uncomfortable situations, misunderstandings, or even harassment. It is crucial to maintain boundaries and ensure a safe and respectful work environment for all employees.

By embracing the concept of erotism in business management, organizations can tap into the immense potential of their workforce. Recognizing and valuing the emotional aspects of individuals can have far-reaching benefits for both employees and the organization as a whole.

One of the key advantages of incorporating erotism in management is the fostering of deeper connections among team members. When individuals are encouraged to express their emotions and passions openly, it creates a sense of psychological safety within the workplace. Employees feel more comfortable sharing their thoughts, ideas, and concerns, which leads to improved communication and collaboration. This, in turn, strengthens interpersonal relationships and builds a sense of trust and camaraderie among colleagues. Deeper connections and enhanced teamwork ultimately contribute to a more harmonious and productive work environment.

Moreover, the recognition and acknowledgement of human desires and aspirations can have a profound impact on employee engagement. When employees feel that their personal passions and interests are valued, they become more motivated to invest their time and energy into their work.

By aligning tasks and projects with individual strengths and interests, managers can create a sense of purpose and meaning for employees, resulting in increased job satisfaction and intrinsic motivation. Engaged employees are more likely to go above and beyond their assigned responsibilities, exhibit higher levels of creativity, and contribute innovative ideas that drive the organization forward.

Furthermore, promoting a work environment that embraces erotism can contribute to a sense of fulfillment for employees. When individuals are encouraged to pursue their passions and find personal meaning in their work, they experience a greater sense of satisfaction and well-being.

This holistic approach to management recognizes that employees are not solely driven by financial rewards but also seek fulfillment and a sense of purpose in their professional lives. By nurturing this aspect of employees' well-being, organizations can create a more positive and fulfilling work culture, leading to improved employee retention, reduced burnout, and enhanced overall job satisfaction.

Additionally, the concept of erotism in business management encourages a broader perspective on employee development. By considering the emotional and personal aspects of individuals, managers can provide tailored opportunities for growth and development.

This may involve providing training and resources that support employees' interests and aspirations or creating avenues for personal and professional development that go beyond traditional job-related skills. By investing in the holistic development of their employees, organizations foster a culture of continuous learning and self-improvement, which not only benefits the individuals but also contributes to the long-term success and competitiveness of the organization.

In conclusion, embracing the concept of erotism in business management goes beyond conventional approaches to managing human resources.

By recognizing and valuing the broader spectrum of human emotions, passions, and desires, organizations can create a dynamic and vibrant work environment that nurtures both personal and professional growth.

Fostering deeper connections, enhancing employee engagement, and promoting a sense of fulfillment and satisfaction are just some of the many advantages that arise from incorporating erotism in management practices.

Ultimately, by prioritizing the emotional well-being and personal aspirations of employees, organizations can unlock the full potential of their workforce and cultivate a culture of creativity, collaboration, and success.

The Power of Seduction in Management

In the arena of business and management, conventional wisdom often touts rationality, consistency, and discipline as the primary drivers of successful leadership. While these factors undoubtedly play an instrumental role in driving organizational success, an exploration into more nuanced aspects of interpersonal relations reveals another powerful, albeit often underappreciated, facet of leadership: seduction.

Traditionally associated with romance, the term 'seduction' may initially seem out of place within the professional context. However, the concept of seduction extends far beyond its romantic implications. When stripped of its sensual connotations, seduction in leadership emerges as the ability to evoke desire, captivate attention, and secure commitment. It involves the capacity to spark interest and engagement, driving individuals to willingly, even eagerly, follow the leader's vision.

This exploration pivots around the notion of personal attractiveness as a vital component of managerial seduction. Personal attractiveness, within this context, transcends physical appearance, delving into the deeper realms of charisma, confidence, and allure. It is about a manager's ability to command attention, inspire loyalty, and influence others—not through autocratic decree or material incentives but through the sheer magnetism of their personality. A manager with personal attractiveness is one who can engage their team on a profound level, compelling their commitment and productivity not just to their roles but to the shared vision of the organization.

However, it is crucial to clarify that personal attractiveness in management is not about conforming to societal standards of beauty. It does not advocate for a superficial, image-focused approach to leadership. Instead, it encourages a deeper, more authentic understanding and enhancement of the unique qualities that make each individual leader captivating in their own way.

This notion places a strong emphasis on self-awareness—the conscious understanding of one's strengths, weaknesses, values, and motivations. A self-aware manager can acknowledge their limitations and leverage their strengths, presenting a realistic, relatable figure to their team members. Self-awareness also facilitates emotional intelligence, another critical aspect of personal attractiveness.

Emotional intelligence, the ability to identify, understand, and manage emotions, enhances a manager's capacity to form meaningful connections with their team. It allows them to empathize with their team members' perspectives, validate their feelings, and respond appropriately to their emotional needs. This emotional connection fosters a sense of trust and respect, strengthening the manager's influence and the team's cohesion.

Moreover, personal attractiveness emphasizes authenticity—the courage to be genuine in one's interactions. Authentic managers do not put on a 'mask' or play a role. Instead, they openly express their thoughts and feelings, encouraging a culture of honesty and transparency. Their authenticity facilitates open communication, encourages mutual respect, and builds trust, all of which are fundamental to a productive work environment.

The combination of self-awareness, emotional intelligence, and authenticity creates a unique form of magnetism that differentiates seductive managers from their counterparts. It is this magnetism that inspires team members and stakeholders to align their efforts with the manager's vision. It galvanizes their commitment and spurs their productivity, ultimately driving the organization towards its goals.

Therefore, the power of seduction in management, encapsulated by the concept of personal attractiveness, is a potent tool for enhancing leadership effectiveness. By fostering self-awareness, emotional intelligence, and authenticity, managers can harness this power to create an engaging, innovative, and productive work environment.

However, this approach to management is not without its challenges. Cultivating personal attractiveness requires introspection, vulnerability, and continuous effort. It involves challenging conventional notions of leadership and embracing a more holistic, human-centric approach. Yet, the benefits of this approach—enhanced team engagement, increased productivity, and a more positive work environment—make it a worthwhile endeavor.

Management, as an art and science of organizing, leading, and coordinating human and material resources towards achieving set objectives, relies significantly on the effectiveness of communication.

Communication, in turn, is the process by which information is passed between individuals through a common system of symbols, signs, or behavior. One could argue that the age-old practice of effective communication, by its very nature, is intrinsically 'seductive'. A careful inspection of the principles and objectives behind seductive communication might, indeed, reveal that we have been employing these methods in management for quite some time.

Seductive communication, in the context of management, is often used to describe a method of communication that effectively captures attention, stirs interest, builds connections, and motivates action. It isn't about manipulation or misleading others but, quite the contrary, about fostering understanding, engagement, and constructive influence.

Seductive communication encompasses aspects such as storytelling, the use of compelling narratives, empathetic and active listening, targeted messaging, and the ability to adapt communication styles to different audiences.

Historically, these aspects have been integral parts of management communication. For instance, management has always necessitated the use of compelling narratives to drive teams towards a common goal. Leaders often share vision and strategy in the form of stories, using the power of a well-structured narrative to align individuals and teams. Such narratives, if crafted effectively, stir emotions and engage employees at a deeper level than simple directives or sterile information sharing.

Similarly, empathetic listening and the ability to tailor communication styles according to the audience have been recognized as vital soft skills in effective management. Leaders who listen actively and empathetically tend to build better rapport with their teams, foster trust, and enhance collaboration. They also demonstrate a better understanding of their team's needs, challenges, and perspectives. This empathetic approach helps in effectively managing change, resolving conflicts, and enhancing team cohesion.

Moreover, the concept of targeted messaging is not new to management. It is a cornerstone of managing diverse teams, where the same message may need to be delivered differently to resonate with different team members. In a global and diverse workforce, it is vital to acknowledge and respect cultural nuances, personal preferences, and communication styles. Leaders have been utilizing these principles, albeit not necessarily under the label of 'seductive communication'.

Despite these examples, it's important to clarify that using seductive communication in management doesn't mean that every interaction is or should be 'seductive'. Instead, it implies that leaders should be aware of these techniques and apply them as and when appropriate. It also doesn't guarantee success, as effective communication is just one aspect of successful management, intertwined with factors like leadership style, organizational culture, and individual team member characteristics.

While the term 'seductive communication' might seem novel, many of its principles and objectives are deeply ingrained in the practice of management. The evolution of communication in management has always inclined towards more engaging, empathetic, and adaptive methods. Thus, in essence, we have been using forms of seductive communication in management, possibly without labeling it as such. Acknowledging this could pave the way for a more conscious application of these principles, which, in turn, could enhance the effectiveness of management communication.

Breaking Taboos: Erotism and Professionalism

As we dive further into the essence of this innovative perspective, we find that breaking taboos in the workplace does not necessitate deviating from a moral compass or ignoring the ethical considerations that should underline any leadership approach. Rather, it encourages the dissolution of unnecessary barriers that hinder expression, creativity, and ultimately, productivity. A managerial stance that embraces the concept of erotism within the bounds of professionalism can thus dismantle prejudices, catalyze fresh ideas, and forge stronger bonds between managers and their teams.

In the context of work dynamics, the incorporation of sensuality can be a powerful catalyst for open dialogue, critical thinking, and problem-solving. Sensuality, defined by its original meaning, pertains to perception, feelings, and the gratification of senses.

When this is translated into a business setting, it encourages an atmosphere where ideas can be communicated freely, and where every team member's input is considered and appreciated. This can significantly improve communication and collaboration, ultimately leading to a more efficient and harmonious working environment.

By establishing an environment wherein seduction is recognized as a tool for fostering engagement and participation, managers encourage employees to become more deeply involved in their tasks. This is not about prompting inappropriate advances, but about creating a compelling aura that engages the team, holds their attention, and keeps them motivated. The power of intrigue and interest that is inherent to seduction can inspire team members to bring their best to the table, boosting performance and productivity.

Moreover, the power of seduction in management allows leaders to demonstrate their charisma and build a sense of trust within their teams. Charisma is an often overlooked quality in leadership discussions, but its significance cannot be overstated. A charismatic leader can ignite enthusiasm, inspire loyalty, and earn the respect of their team. Such leaders use their personal appeal, or their 'seductive' qualities, to connect with their team on a deeper level and influence them positively.

In understanding the power of seduction in leadership, it is essential to consider the role of empathy. Empathy, the ability to understand and share the feelings of others, is at the heart of an effective seductive leadership style. A leader who exhibits empathy understands the needs, desires, and concerns of their team, making them feel valued and respected. This fosters a sense of belonging and commitment among team members, enhancing team cohesiveness and performance.

A critical point to note is that while erotism in leadership can offer numerous benefits, it must always be employed with the utmost respect for each individual's personal boundaries and consent. Sensitivity towards cultural, gender, and individual differences is paramount in preventing any potential misunderstandings or discomfort. Leaders who wish to harness the power of seduction in their management approach must be vigilant in ensuring that they promote a culture that respects diversity, champions inclusivity, and safeguards the dignity of all team members.

As we delve deeper into the implications of adopting seduction as a managerial tool, we find that it is about transcending traditional leadership styles and fostering a dynamic, engaging, and empowering work environment. It promotes the idea that work should not be seen as a chore or merely a means to an end, but as an engaging activity that stimulates the mind, fulfills personal goals, and nourishes professional growth. In this manner, the adoption of an erotic leadership style can contribute significantly to employee satisfaction, retention, and overall organizational success.

In conclusion, the interplay between erotism and professionalism in the context of leadership can be a potent force in driving organizational success. It calls for a shift in perspective and a bold approach to management, breaking taboos, and embracing the power of seduction as a tool for cultivating a dynamic, innovative, and highly productive work environment.

While the concept might appear unconventional, its potential benefits underscore the importance of continually challenging the status quo and exploring new strategies for success in the evolving world of business. Through this understanding, managers and leaders can push the boundaries of traditional leadership paradigms and unlock the immense potential that lies within their teams, leading their organizations towards unprecedented heights of success.

Integrating erotism within the realm of professionalism is an attempt to reframe the very foundations of corporate communication and interaction. It's about building a culture where employees feel genuinely connected, excited, and engaged with their work and where leaders use their charisma, empathy, and emotional intelligence to inspire, motivate, and lead.

The dynamic nature of the contemporary work environment demands that we constantly challenge and reinvent traditional management styles. Managers and leaders need to be attuned to the diverse and evolving needs of their teams. They need to create a workplace culture where individuals feel valued and are inspired to perform to the best of their abilities. This is where the concept of erotic leadership or seductive management could add value.

The process involves creating a shared vision and fostering an environment where everyone is comfortable expressing their views and ideas, and where intellectual and emotional connections are built and nurtured. It's about harnessing the power of seduction to fuel engagement, motivation, and productivity.

However, as we integrate elements of sensuality into management, it's important to maintain a balance between being engaging and overstepping boundaries. Sensuality here is not about sexual appeal but about engaging people's senses, stirring their emotions, and connecting on a more personal level. It's about making the workplace a more vibrant, passionate, and lively place where employees feel a sense of belonging and camaraderie.

The power of erotism in management lies not in explicitness but in subtlety and finesse. It's about creating an environment of trust and respect where everyone feels valued and heard. It's about using charisma, emotional intelligence, and effective communication to captivate attention, inspire action, and cultivate a motivated, high-performing team.

At the same time, it is crucial to recognize that while erotism and professionalism can coexist and complement each other, they must be handled with sensitivity and respect. Managers and leaders need to be mindful of cultural and individual sensitivities and always uphold the principles of respect, dignity, and consent. They need to ensure that they are not crossing any personal boundaries and that their actions are not perceived as inappropriate or uncomfortable.

In the end, embracing erotism in the professional sphere is about reimagining the traditional workplace. It's about fostering a culture of engagement, motivation, and innovation. It's about transforming the mundane into the exciting and the ordinary into the extraordinary. It's about breaking down barriers, challenging the status quo, and harnessing the power of seduction to drive organizational success.

But as we navigate this new landscape of management, we need to tread with caution. We need to remember that while erotism can be a powerful tool for engagement and motivation, it must always be employed with respect and consideration for individual boundaries and comfort levels. Only then can we truly unlock its potential and reap the benefits that it offers.

The Role of Erotism in the Business Environment

In the business world, where logic, strategy, and data-driven decision-making dominate, the idea of incorporating erotism may initially seem unconventional or even taboo. However, upon closer examination, it becomes apparent that erotism can play a significant role in fostering a thriving and dynamic business environment. This analysis aims to delve into the multifaceted aspects of erotism within the business context and explore its potential impact on various facets of organizational functioning.

Erotism, when applied judiciously and ethically, has the power to transform the way individuals interact, communicate, and collaborate within an organization.

At its core, erotism involves tapping into the sensual, passionate, and deeply human aspects of individuals. By acknowledging and embracing these elements, managers can create an environment that encourages creativity, stimulates innovation, and fosters authentic human connections.

One of the fundamental aspects of incorporating erotism in the business environment is recognizing and celebrating the diverse range of human desires and emotions. In a world that often compartmentalizes personal and professional lives, acknowledging and integrating these dimensions can lead to a more holistic and fulfilling work experience. When employees are allowed to express their passions, desires, and emotions in a healthy and respectful manner, they are more likely to feel engaged, motivated, and empowered.

Erotism can also contribute to breaking down traditional hierarchical structures within organizations. By promoting open and transparent communication channels, individuals are encouraged to express their desires, needs, and concerns.

This openness fosters a culture of trust, mutual respect, and collaboration, allowing for more fluid and dynamic exchanges of ideas and perspectives. As a result, innovative solutions can emerge, and the organization as a whole can adapt more effectively to a rapidly changing business landscape.

Moreover, the integration of erotism in the business environment can have a positive impact on employee well-being and satisfaction. When individuals are encouraged to embrace their sensual and passionate sides, they are more likely to experience a sense of fulfillment and authenticity in their work.

This, in turn, can lead to increased levels of motivation, productivity, and loyalty. By creating a work environment that values and nurtures the holistic well-being of its employees, organizations can attract and retain top talent, fostering a competitive advantage in the market.

When it comes to leadership, incorporating elements of erotism can redefine the traditional notions of authority and influence. Instead of relying solely on traditional power dynamics, leaders who embrace erotism understand the importance of emotional intelligence, empathy, and authentic connection. By cultivating an atmosphere of mutual desire, trust, and vulnerability, leaders can inspire and motivate their teams on a deeper level, unlocking their full potential.

However, it is important to note that the integration of erotism in the business environment requires a nuanced understanding of boundaries, consent, and ethical considerations. While erotism can be a powerful force for positive change, it should never be used to exploit or manipulate individuals.

Managers and leaders must be attentive to the potential risks and challenges associated with incorporating erotism in the workplace. Clear guidelines, open communication, and a strong ethical framework should be established to ensure that all interactions and practices are consensual, respectful, and aligned with organizational values.

The role of erotism in the business environment extends far beyond its initial perception as a taboo or unconventional concept. When applied with sensitivity, ethics, and a deep understanding of human desires and emotions, erotism can revolutionize the way organizations operate.

By embracing and celebrating the sensual, passionate, and authentic aspects of human nature, managers can create a workplace that is more engaging, innovative, and fulfilling. The integration of erotism in the business environment has the potential to transform organizational culture, enhance employee well-being and satisfaction, and unleash untapped creative potential.

By incorporating erotism, managers can encourage employees to fully express their passions and desires, leading to a more fulfilling work experience. This can be achieved by creating an environment that values the diverse range of human emotions and allows individuals to explore their sensual sides without fear of judgment or reprisal. By embracing erotism, organizations can tap into a deep well of creativity, as employees feel inspired and empowered to bring their whole selves to work.

In addition to promoting individual well-being, the integration of erotism in the business environment can foster stronger relationships and enhance collaboration among team members. When individuals are encouraged to express their desires and needs openly, it creates a culture of trust and mutual respect.

This, in turn, leads to more effective communication and the free exchange of ideas. By removing the barriers to authentic expression, organizations can unlock the full potential of their workforce and drive innovation.

Furthermore, erotism can challenge traditional hierarchical structures and power dynamics within organizations. Instead of relying solely on positional authority, leaders who embrace erotism understand the importance of emotional intelligence and empathic connection.

They create an environment where individuals feel valued, seen, and understood. This inclusive approach to leadership fosters a sense of belonging and encourages collaboration, ultimately leading to higher employee engagement and productivity.

However, it is essential to approach the integration of erotism with caution and respect for ethical boundaries. Consent, transparency, and open communication are vital in ensuring that all interactions and practices are consensual and respectful.

Organizations must establish clear guidelines and codes of conduct to prevent any misuse or exploitation of the power dynamics associated with erotism. By setting these boundaries, organizations can create a safe and empowering environment for their employees to explore their desires and passions.

Additionally, it is crucial to acknowledge that the concept of erotism can be subjective and culturally influenced. What may be considered erotic in one culture or context may not be the same in another. Therefore, organizations should take into account the cultural diversity of their workforce and be sensitive to different perspectives and comfort levels. By fostering an inclusive environment that respects and celebrates diverse expressions of erotism, organizations can create a sense of belonging and ensure that all employees feel valued and respected.

In conclusion, the integration of erotism in the business environment has the potential to transform organizational culture and enhance employee well-being and satisfaction. By embracing and celebrating the sensual and passionate aspects of human nature, organizations can create a work environment that encourages creativity, innovation, and authentic connections. However, it is crucial to approach the integration of erotism with care, ensuring that ethical boundaries are respected and that all employees feel safe and respected in expressing their desires and passions. By doing so, organizations can create a workplace that is vibrant, engaging, and conducive to personal and professional growth.

The concept of erotism, when introduced and applied strategically in a professional setting, has the potential to shift the paradigm of how we view communication, collaboration, and leadership within an organization.

This perspective represents a radical departure from traditional business practices that often privilege logic, strategy, and data-driven decision-making. Instead, it calls for a nuanced understanding and appreciation of the myriad emotions, desires, and passions that drive human behavior.

Implementing erotism in a professional context can help foster an environment that encourages creativity and innovation. It can create a space where individuals feel comfortable expressing their deepest desires and passions, fostering an atmosphere where novel ideas can be generated and explored freely. This could lead to a more enriching, stimulating, and ultimately, rewarding work experience for everyone involved.

Moreover, the infusion of erotism within a professional setting can help redefine the relationships and dynamics within a team. Traditional hierarchical structures may begin to morph into more fluid and flexible networks of communication. The openness and transparency that comes with the acceptance of the concept of erotism can breed a culture of trust, empathy, and mutual respect, fostering a healthier and more collaborative environment.

An erotically charged work environment may also contribute positively to the well-being and satisfaction of employees. Encouraging employees to embrace their sensual and passionate selves can boost their self-confidence and create a sense of authenticity and fulfillment in their roles. It can lead to increased motivation, commitment, and productivity, and over time, contribute to an organization's competitive advantage.

From a leadership perspective, embracing erotism can provide a new lens through which to exercise authority and influence. Instead of relying solely on power dynamics inherent in traditional leadership models, leaders can use elements of erotism to connect with their teams on a deeper, more emotional level. This approach to leadership can engender a sense of unity, commitment, and motivation, enabling teams to perform to their highest potential.

However, the incorporation of erotism within the business environment is not without its challenges. Ethical considerations must be at the forefront when implementing such an approach. The potential for misuse or exploitation cannot be overlooked, and measures must be put in place to ensure that erotism is used ethically and responsibly. This includes setting clear boundaries, ensuring consent, and fostering an environment where open and honest communication is the norm.

Furthermore, it is vital to bear in mind that perceptions and interpretations of erotism can vary greatly among individuals, influenced by cultural norms, personal beliefs, and past experiences. Therefore, a one-size-fits-all approach will not suffice. Leaders need to be sensitive to these differences and ensure that their use of erotism respects the comfort levels and boundaries of all team members.

In conclusion, while the concept of erotism in the business context may seem unconventional at first glance, it has the potential to bring about significant positive change in organizational dynamics and performance. It encourages an environment of openness, creativity, and innovation, fosters a more engaged and satisfied workforce, and provides leaders with a new approach to exercise their influence.

However, as said before, the implementation of such a strategy must be done with caution, ensuring that the principles of respect, consent, and ethical conduct guide every interaction. With these measures in place, the benefits of integrating erotism within the business environment can be fully realized.

Personal Attractiveness as a Leadership Tool

In the realm of leadership, personal attractiveness holds a significant role as a powerful tool for influencing and inspiring others. It goes beyond superficial appearance and delves into the realm of charisma, confidence, and allure.

A leader who exudes personal attractiveness can command attention, inspire loyalty, and effortlessly influence others. This chapter aims to explore the multifaceted aspects of personal attractiveness as a leadership tool and its potential impact on various aspects of organizational dynamics.

When discussing the concept of personal attractiveness in leadership, it is essential to underscore the multi-faceted nature of this construct. Attractiveness, particularly in the context of leadership, isn't a singular, dimensional trait but rather an amalgamation of distinctive attributes that evoke a sense of connection, respect, and admiration in others.

Indeed, the allure of a leader, the magnetic pull that inspires followership, cannot be reduced to the simplicity of physical aesthetics. Instead, it is their charisma, self-confidence, authenticity, and emotional intelligence that form the very fabric of their allure.

Charisma, the compelling charm that inspires devotion in others, is a quality synonymous with influential leaders. A charismatic leader radiates a certain level of energy and optimism that is infectious, arousing enthusiasm and commitment among their team members.

The charismatic leader's aura isn't a product of physical attractiveness but stems from their ability to articulate a compelling vision, their confidence, their assertiveness, and, above all, their unwavering belief in the capabilities of their team. This charisma, this irresistible magnetism, makes them a beacon that others are naturally drawn to, stimulating loyalty, motivation, and a strong drive to perform.

However, charisma without self-confidence would be like a ship without a compass. Self-confidence is the sturdy foundation upon which charismatic leadership stands. A self-confident leader exudes a strong sense of self-assuredness and resilience, which instills confidence in others. It is their belief in their abilities, their unwavering faith in the face of challenges, and their willingness to take risks that makes them stand out. Their conviction becomes the team's conviction, their strength becomes the team's strength, and this collective faith and resilience drive the team towards success.

The role of emotional intelligence in personal attractiveness cannot be overstated. An emotionally intelligent leader is someone who is not only aware of their own emotions but also empathetic towards the feelings of others. They are able to manage their emotions in a healthy manner and use this emotional awareness to guide their decision-making process. Emotionally intelligent leaders foster an environment of psychological safety, where team members feel comfortable expressing their feelings and ideas. This ability to connect with others on an emotional level is a powerful tool in building strong, cohesive teams.

Indeed, the ability to form deep connections with others is the linchpin that holds all these qualities together. When a leader is able to genuinely connect with their team members, to understand their aspirations, their fears, and their motivations, they are able to inspire them to perform at their best. They are able to create an environment where individuals feel valued, understood, and motivated to contribute towards the collective vision.

Personal attractiveness in leadership is a complex amalgamation of charisma, self-confidence, authenticity, emotional intelligence, and the ability to form deep connections. It is these qualities that form the very essence of an attractive leader, the magnetic pull that draws individuals towards them and inspires trust and admiration.

It's not the physical beauty, but the beauty of these inherent traits, that truly makes a leader attractive and influential. It is a powerful testament to the idea that real attractiveness transcends physical aesthetics, residing instead in the unique qualities that a leader brings to the table. This understanding redefines the concept of personal attractiveness in leadership, placing the focus on the intangible yet impactful attributes that inspire followership, drive performance, and ultimately lead to success.

Authenticity is another key element of personal attractiveness. Authentic leaders are genuine and true to themselves, which creates a sense of trust and credibility among their followers. When leaders are authentic, they are able to connect with others on a deeper level, as their actions and words align with their values and beliefs. This authenticity resonates with others, making them more likely to trust and follow the leader's guidance.

Confidence is another attribute that contributes to personal attractiveness as a leadership tool. Confidence enables leaders to project a sense of certainty and competence, inspiring confidence in their abilities.

When leaders exude confidence, they instill a sense of assurance in their team members, who look to them for guidance and direction. Confidence also encourages risk-taking and innovation, as team members feel empowered to explore new ideas and approaches under the guidance of a confident leader.

The ability to connect with others on a deeper level is a distinguishing characteristic of attractive leaders. Personal attractiveness involves creating genuine and meaningful connections with team members.

This connection is built on trust, empathy, and active listening. Leaders who actively listen and show genuine interest in their team members' perspectives and concerns foster an environment of psychological safety, where individuals feel valued and motivated to contribute their best.

When personal attractiveness is leveraged effectively, it can have a transformative impact on organizational dynamics. Attractive leaders have the ability to inspire and motivate their teams to achieve exceptional results. Their magnetic presence and influential demeanor can create a positive work culture characterized by high levels of engagement, collaboration, and innovation. Employees are more likely to be loyal, committed, and dedicated when they feel inspired and valued by their attractive leaders.

However, it is important to note that personal attractiveness as a leadership tool should be approached with authenticity and integrity. It should never be used manipulatively or exploitatively. Leaders should strive to enhance their personal attractiveness by developing their character, honing their communication skills, and cultivating a genuine interest in the well-being and growth of their team members.

Authenticity is paramount, as followers are more likely to recognize and respond positively to leaders who genuinely care about their success and create an environment that fosters their personal and professional development.

Personal attractiveness holds a significant role as a leadership tool. It encompasses charisma, authenticity, emotional intelligence, confidence, and the ability to connect with others on a deeper level. When leaders possess these qualities, they become influential figures who inspire and motivate their teams.

Personal attractiveness can transform organizational dynamics, creating a positive work culture characterized by high levels of engagement, collaboration, and innovation. However, it is crucial for leaders to approach personal attractiveness with authenticity and integrity, ensuring that their actions align with their values and genuine concern for the well-being of their team members.

There have been several business and political leaders throughout history who have utilized their personal attractiveness to succeed in their careers. Here are some notable examples:

Richard Branson: The charismatic and adventurous founder of Virgin Group, Richard Branson, has leveraged his personal attractiveness to build a vast business empire. Known for his larger-than-life personality, Branson's charm, confidence, and adventurous spirit have helped him establish successful ventures in various industries, including music, airlines, telecommunications, and space travel.

Oprah Winfrey: As one of the most influential media moguls in the world, Oprah Winfrey has used her personal attractiveness to connect with audiences and build an empire. Her authenticity, empathy, and ability to connect with people on an emotional level have made her a trusted and beloved figure. Through her talk shows, media ventures, and philanthropic efforts, Winfrey has achieved remarkable success and garnered a loyal following.

Barack Obama: Former U.S. President Barack Obama is often regarded as a charismatic leader who utilized his personal attractiveness to connect with voters and inspire a sense of hope and change. His eloquence, charisma, and ability to connect with diverse audiences played a significant role in his political rise and his ability to rally support during his presidency.

Angela Merkel: As the Chancellor of Germany for 16 years, Angela Merkel demonstrated the power of personal attractiveness in the political realm. While not traditionally seen as charismatic in the conventional sense, Merkel's pragmatic approach, steady leadership, and calm demeanor resonated with many Germans. Her ability to inspire confidence and stability in times of crisis contributed to her long-lasting political success.

Elon Musk: The visionary entrepreneur and CEO of companies like Tesla and SpaceX, Elon Musk, has gained attention for his personal attractiveness and magnetic presence. Musk's confidence, ambition, and ability to communicate his grand visions have captivated the public's imagination. His personal brand has become synonymous with innovation and disruption, making him a highly influential figure in the business world.

Jacinda Ardern: As the Prime Minister of New Zealand, Jacinda Ardern has been praised for her personal attractiveness and leadership style. Ardern's empathetic and compassionate approach, particularly in times of crisis, has resonated with people both within New Zealand and around the world. Her ability to connect with individuals on a human level has contributed to her popularity and success as a political leader.

These are just a few examples of business and political leaders who have used their personal attractiveness to succeed in their careers. Each leader has leveraged their unique qualities, such as charisma, authenticity, empathy, and confidence, to connect with others, inspire trust, and achieve remarkable accomplishments in their respective fields.

Breaking Taboos: Erotism and Professionalism

In the realm of management, there exists a delicate balance between the professional and the personal. Traditionally, the workplace has been seen as a space where strict adherence to professionalism is expected, and the expression of personal desires or sexuality is considered inappropriate.

However, in recent years, there has been a growing recognition of the potential benefits of breaking taboos and incorporating elements of erotism into the business environment. This chapter aims to explore the complex interplay between erotica and professionalism, examining the challenges, opportunities, and ethical considerations associated with this unconventional approach.

To begin our exploration, it is essential to define what we mean by "breaking taboos" in the context of erotica and professionalism. Breaking taboos refers to challenging and subverting societal norms and expectations regarding the expression of desire, sensuality, and sexuality within the workplace.

It involves embracing the notion that human beings are multifaceted individuals with desires and emotions that extend beyond the confines of traditional professionalism. By breaking these taboos, managers can create an environment that encourages authenticity, emotional expression, and open-mindedness.

The integration of erotica and professionalism raises important questions regarding boundaries, consent, and ethics. It is crucial to establish clear guidelines and communication channels to ensure that all interactions and practices are consensual, respectful, and aligned with organizational values. The respect for personal boundaries and the recognition of diverse comfort levels are paramount in maintaining a safe and inclusive work environment.

One potential benefit of breaking taboos and incorporating elements of erotism in the workplace is the stimulation of creativity and innovation. By encouraging individuals to explore and express their desires and sensuality within ethical boundaries, organizations can tap into a deeper well of human potential.

Erotism has the potential to unlock unconventional perspectives, inspire risk-taking, and challenge the status quo. When employees feel safe and empowered to express their desires and passions, they are more likely to think outside the box, leading to fresh ideas and novel solutions.

Moreover, breaking taboos can also foster a more inclusive and diverse work environment. By embracing erotica and challenging societal norms, organizations send a powerful message of acceptance and respect for individual differences.

This can create a culture that values diversity of expression, allowing employees to bring their whole selves to work. When individuals feel accepted and valued for who they are, regardless of their sexual orientation or gender identity, they are more likely to thrive, contribute, and form strong connections with their colleagues.

However, it is essential to recognize and address the potential risks and challenges associated with breaking taboos in the workplace. While the integration of erotism can have positive outcomes, it also requires a thoughtful and responsible approach. Managers must be vigilant in identifying and addressing any instances of harassment, exploitation, or power imbalances that may arise. This necessitates fostering a culture of open communication, providing training on boundaries and consent, and establishing clear channels for reporting and addressing concerns.

Ethical considerations are also paramount in the integration of erotica and professionalism. The use of erotic elements should never be manipulative or exploitative, and consent should always be actively sought and respected.

Managers must ensure that employees have the freedom to opt-in or opt-out of any activities or initiatives related to erotism. Furthermore, it is important to strike a balance between promoting an environment that embraces sensuality and desire while maintaining professionalism and respect for all individuals involved.

An additional challenge to consider is the potential impact on organizational reputation. While breaking taboos and embracing erotica may have positive effects within the workplace, organizations must be mindful of external perceptions and cultural sensitivities. Public perception and societal expectations vary widely, and what may be acceptable in one context could be met with disapproval or controversy in another. It is crucial for organizations to consider the potential impact on their brand image, stakeholders, and customers before implementing any initiatives related to erotica.

On the other hand, breaking taboos and integrating elements of erotism can bring significant benefits to the workplace. By challenging the status quo and embracing a more open and accepting environment, organizations can foster a culture of authenticity, trust, and empowerment.

When employees feel free to express their desires and sensuality in a respectful and consensual manner, it can lead to increased engagement, motivation, and satisfaction. This, in turn, can have a positive impact on productivity, collaboration, and overall organizational performance.

Furthermore, breaking taboos and incorporating elements of erotism can also enhance communication and interpersonal dynamics within teams. When individuals feel safe and accepted in expressing their desires and emotions, it creates an environment of psychological safety.

This encourages open and honest communication, leading to more effective collaboration and problem-solving. In addition, the integration of erotism can promote a greater sense of empathy and understanding among team members, as they are encouraged to consider and respect the desires and boundaries of others.

Another aspect to consider is the impact of breaking taboos on employee well-being and mental health. By creating a space where individuals can freely express their desires and sensuality, organizations can contribute to a greater sense of self-acceptance and personal growth. This can lead to increased self-esteem and overall well-being, as employees are encouraged to embrace and celebrate their authentic selves. When employees feel supported and accepted for who they are, it creates a positive work environment that fosters both personal and professional development.

In addition, breaking taboos and incorporating elements of erotism can positively impact diversity and inclusion efforts within organizations. By creating an environment that embraces a range of expressions and desires, organizations send a message of acceptance and respect for individual differences.

This can attract a diverse workforce and contribute to a more inclusive culture where all employees feel valued and celebrated for their unique identities and experiences. When employees feel a sense of belonging, it enhances engagement, retention, and overall organizational success.

While breaking taboos and integrating elements of erotism can offer significant benefits, it is essential to consider the potential challenges and drawbacks. Organizations must approach this approach with caution and sensitivity, taking into account the cultural context, legal considerations, and the diverse perspectives and comfort levels of their employees. It is crucial to establish clear guidelines and policies to ensure that all interactions and practices are consensual, respectful, and aligned with organizational values.

Moreover, it is essential to provide education and training to employees and leaders on topics such as boundaries, consent, and respectful communication. This can help foster a culture of understanding, empathy, and mutual respect, ensuring that all individuals feel safe and empowered within the workplace.

In summary, breaking taboos and incorporating elements of erotism into the business environment is a complex endeavor that requires careful consideration, open communication, and ethical awareness.

While it offers opportunities for increased creativity, diversity, and authenticity, it also poses challenges related to boundaries, consent, and potential reputational risks. By creating a safe and inclusive environment that respects personal boundaries and encourages open dialogue, organizations can navigate the delicate balance between erotica and professionalism.

The responsible integration of erotism can lead to a more vibrant, innovative, and inclusive workplace where individuals feel empowered to express their authentic selves and contribute their fullest potential to the organization.

The Seductive Communication

Effective communication is a cornerstone of successful leadership. It is through communication that leaders inspire, motivate, and influence their teams to achieve shared goals.

In recent years, there has been a growing recognition of the power of seductive communication in the business world. Seductive communication involves using persuasive techniques that captivate and engage the audience, creating a compelling and irresistible message.

This section aims to explore the multifaceted aspects of seductive communication and its impact on leadership effectiveness. Additionally, we will examine contemporary examples of business leaders who have effectively utilized seductive communication to achieve their goals.

Seductive communication goes beyond conventional communication techniques by tapping into emotions, desires, and the psychological triggers of the audience.

It aims to create an emotional connection and capture the attention of listeners through the use of language, storytelling, body language, and non-verbal cues. The goal is to engage the audience on a deeper level, arousing curiosity, desire, and a sense of urgency to act.

One powerful aspect of seductive communication is the use of storytelling. Leaders who employ storytelling techniques can weave narratives that evoke emotions and create a memorable and engaging experience for their audience.

By sharing personal anecdotes, case studies, or relatable experiences, leaders can captivate their listeners and inspire them to action. Stories have a unique ability to engage both the logical and emotional faculties of the brain, making them a powerful tool for persuasion.

For example, Steve Jobs, the late co-founder of Apple, was known for his ability to use storytelling to convey the vision and purpose of Apple products during his iconic product launch events. His captivating narratives created excitement and anticipation among Apple enthusiasts, driving demand and market success.

When unveiling the iPhone in 2007, Jobs used a storytelling approach, painting a vivid picture of the device's revolutionary features and how it would transform the way people communicate. This seductive communication style allowed Jobs to not only introduce a product but also create an emotional connection with the audience, leading to a fervent desire to own the groundbreaking technology.

Another element of seductive communication is the skillful use of language. Leaders who possess a charismatic and seductive communication style choose their words carefully to evoke emotions, create imagery, and spark desire.

By employing vivid and persuasive language, they can paint a compelling picture of their ideas, products, or services. The choice of words can influence how a message is received, as certain phrases or expressions have the power to elicit strong emotions or convey a sense of urgency.

Elon Musk, the CEO of Tesla and SpaceX, is known for his charismatic communication style. He uses bold and imaginative language to describe his ambitious plans for space exploration and sustainable energy, capturing the attention and imagination of his audience.

When discussing the mission of SpaceX to colonize Mars, Musk has referred to it as a "multiplanetary species insurance policy" and "making life multiplanetary." These carefully crafted expressions resonate with his audience's desire for exploration and progress, creating a seductive allure around his vision and generating excitement and support for his ventures.

Body language and non-verbal cues play a crucial role in seductive communication. Leaders who are aware of their body language can enhance their message and create a captivating presence. They use gestures, facial expressions, and eye contact to convey confidence, authenticity, and passion. These non-verbal cues can significantly impact how a message is received, as they convey emotions and establish a connection with the audience.

Sheryl Sandberg, the former COO of Facebook, is recognized for her charismatic and seductive communication style. Her confident body language, warm smile, and engaging eye contact create a powerful connection with her audience, making her a compelling and influential speaker. Sandberg's ability to combine her body language with persuasive language allows her to convey her messages with impact and authenticity. Her TED Talk on "Why We Have Too Few Women Leaders" exemplifies her seductive communication style, as she uses a combination of personal anecdotes, emotional appeals, and confident body language to engage and inspire her audience.

In the digital age, seductive communication has expanded to include virtual platforms and social media. Business leaders leverage these platforms to engage with their audience and convey their message in a seductive manner. They utilize visually appealing graphics, compelling videos, and captivating storytelling techniques to capture attention and create an emotional impact. The use of visuals, such as eye-catching images or videos, can enhance the seductive appeal of the message and leave a lasting impression on the audience.

Gary Vaynerchuk, a renowned entrepreneur and social media influencer, effectively uses online platforms to engage and motivate his followers. His energetic and seductive communication style, combined with relatable and impactful content, has gained him a large and dedicated following. Through his social media channels, Vaynerchuk employs various seductive communication techniques, such as sharing personal stories, leveraging powerful visuals, and using persuasive language to inspire action and create a sense of urgency.

While seductive communication can be a powerful tool for business leaders, it is essential to use it ethically and responsibly. Leaders must maintain authenticity, integrity, and respect for their audience.

The intent should be to genuinely connect and inspire, rather than manipulate or deceive. The goal of seductive communication is not to exploit emotions for personal gain but to create an emotional resonance that aligns with the shared goals and values of both the leader and the audience.

Additionally, leaders must be mindful of cultural differences and adapt their communication style accordingly, ensuring that their message is appropriate and resonates with diverse audiences. Different cultures have varying norms, sensitivities, and interpretations of seductive communication. Leaders must be sensitive to these differences and tailor their approach to maintain cultural appropriateness and avoid unintended consequences.

In conclusion, seductive communication has emerged as a compelling approach for business leaders to captivate and engage their audience. Through storytelling, persuasive language, body language, and non-verbal cues, leaders can create emotional connections, inspire action, and achieve their goals.

The examples of Steve Jobs, Elon Musk, Sheryl Sandberg, and Gary Vaynerchuk demonstrate the effectiveness of seductive communication when employed authentically and responsibly. By harnessing the power of seductive communication, leaders can communicate their vision, influence their teams, and drive success in the business world.

Looking forward, as our world becomes increasingly digital, the role of seductive communication will continue to evolve. The use of emerging technologies, such as virtual reality, augmented reality, and AI-driven platforms, offer novel ways to captivate and engage audiences. However, as with all communication methods, the effectiveness of these new tools will largely depend on how well leaders understand their audiences' desires, needs, and emotional triggers.

Moreover, in a world of increasing information overload, the ability to stand out and capture attention becomes all the more crucial. Leaders must not only be able to communicate their message effectively, but they must also do so in a way that is unique, memorable, and resonates with their audience on an emotional level.

Leaders who succeed in mastering the art of seductive communication can inspire their teams to exceed their limits, rally support for their vision, and motivate stakeholders to take action. Whether through a compelling narrative, captivating language, powerful body language, or immersive digital content, seductive communication can be a potent tool for driving organizational success.

In the ever-evolving landscape of business leadership, the ability to adapt and innovate in communication strategies will be key to maintaining influence and achieving goals. The examples of Jobs, Musk, Sandberg, and Vaynerchuk show that harnessing the power of seductive communication can create a lasting impact, both on individuals and on the wider business landscape.

However, it is essential to note that seductive communication is not about manipulation, but about creating meaningful connections. The goal is to inspire, motivate, and engage, not to deceive or exploit. As leaders navigate the complexities of seductive communication, they must remain committed to ethical practices, demonstrating respect and consideration for their audiences.

Overall, the future of leadership communication is exciting and dynamic, with ample opportunities for leaders to harness the power of seductive communication to inspire and drive success. By continuously learning and adapting, today's leaders can create meaningful and impactful messages that resonate deeply with their audiences, fostering an environment of mutual understanding, shared goals, and collective achievement.

The Importance of Nonverbal Communication

Nonverbal communication, often referred to as body language, plays a vital role in how we convey messages, establish connections, and influence others. It encompasses a wide range of cues, including facial expressions, gestures, posture, eye contact, and tone of voice. While verbal communication focuses on the spoken word, nonverbal cues can significantly impact the effectiveness and interpretation of our messages.

This section aims to explore the importance of nonverbal communication in various contexts, including politics and business, and highlight examples of politicians and business leaders who effectively utilize nonverbal communication to enhance their messages.

Nonverbal communication serves as a powerful supplement to verbal communication, as it can reinforce, emphasize, or even contradict the spoken words. It provides additional layers of meaning, emotional cues, and context that enrich the overall message being conveyed. Understanding and effectively utilizing nonverbal cues can significantly enhance communication outcomes, leading to improved rapport, trust, and comprehension between individuals.

One area where nonverbal communication plays a prominent role is in politics. Political leaders rely heavily on their nonverbal cues to connect with audiences, convey confidence, and inspire trust. They often employ gestures, facial expressions, and body language to enhance the impact of their speeches and public appearances. Nonverbal cues can help politicians convey authenticity, establish credibility, and create an emotional connection with their constituents.

We refer again to Barack Obama, the 44th President of the United States, was known for his ability to use nonverbal communication to convey his messages effectively. His calm and composed demeanor, combined with confident body language and measured hand gestures, projected a sense of authority and trustworthiness. Obama's use of nonverbal cues, such as maintaining eye contact with his audience and displaying open and welcoming gestures, allowed him to establish a connection and build rapport with people from diverse backgrounds.

In the business world, nonverbal communication is equally crucial. Successful business leaders recognize the significance of nonverbal cues in conveying their intentions, building rapport, and influencing others.

They understand that nonverbal communication can either reinforce their message or undermine it, depending on how it is used. Nonverbal cues can help business leaders establish their presence, convey confidence, and enhance their persuasive abilities.

Indra Nooyi, the former CEO of PepsiCo, is an example of a business leader who effectively utilizes nonverbal communication. Nooyi's strong presence, confident posture, and engaging eye contact project her leadership qualities and reinforce her messages during public appearances and interviews. Her use of nonverbal cues, such as purposeful hand gestures and expressive facial expressions, enhances the impact of her communication and creates a lasting impression.

Furthermore, Jeff Bezos, the founder and former CEO of Amazon, is known for his use of nonverbal cues to communicate his vision and passion. Bezos' animated and enthusiastic delivery, combined with his energetic body language and gestures, conveys his excitement and commitment to his ideas. His nonverbal cues create an aura of enthusiasm and inspire his employees and stakeholders to share in his vision and dedication.

Nonverbal communication can reinforce a message by aligning with and enhancing the spoken words. When nonverbal cues are congruent with the verbal message, they create a sense of coherence and credibility.

For example, imagine a business leader discussing the importance of teamwork and collaboration while using open gestures, maintaining eye contact, and displaying a relaxed and approachable demeanor. These nonverbal cues support the verbal message and convey the leader's commitment to collaboration, thereby reinforcing the overall message.

Conversely, nonverbal cues can also unintentionally contradict or undermine the spoken message if they are incongruent or misaligned. Inconsistencies between verbal and nonverbal cues can create confusion, mistrust, and a sense of dissonance.

For instance, if a politician delivers a speech on environmental sustainability but exhibits closed body language, lack of eye contact, and a disinterested facial expression, the nonverbal cues may signal insincerity or lack of conviction, undermining the message's credibility and impact.

In addition to reinforcing the spoken message, nonverbal communication can also help clarify and emphasize key points. Leaders can use nonverbal cues such as gestures, intonation, and facial expressions to highlight important ideas and create a sense of emphasis. These nonverbal cues draw attention to specific elements of the message, making it more memorable and impactful for the audience.

On the other hand, nonverbal cues can also play a destructive role in communication if not used effectively. Inappropriate or offensive nonverbal behavior can undermine trust, create discomfort, and damage relationships.

For example, crossing one's arms during a conversation can signal defensiveness or resistance, hindering effective communication and creating a barrier between the speaker and the listener. It is crucial for leaders to be aware of their nonverbal cues and ensure they align with the intended message and the desired outcome.

Effective nonverbal communication involves self-awareness, adaptability, and the ability to read and respond to others' nonverbal cues. It requires paying attention to one's own body language and being attuned to the nonverbal signals of others. By actively listening and observing, individuals can better understand the emotions, attitudes, and intentions of those they interact with, leading to improved communication outcomes.

Politicians and business leaders must also be mindful of cultural differences in nonverbal communication. Gestures, facial expressions, and body language can carry different meanings across cultures.

Leaders who operate in diverse contexts need to familiarize themselves with cultural norms to avoid unintentionally conveying inappropriate or offensive messages. Adapting nonverbal cues to align with cultural sensitivities demonstrates respect and helps establish rapport with individuals from different backgrounds.

In conclusion, nonverbal communication is a vital component of effective communication in various domains, including politics and business. It provides essential cues that enrich the meaning of verbal messages, evoke emotions, and establish connections between individuals.

Politicians and business leaders who effectively utilize nonverbal communication can reinforce their messages, inspire trust, and connect with their audiences on a deeper level. However, it is essential to remain mindful of the potential impact of nonverbal cues, as they can either enhance or undermine the intended message.

By understanding the importance of nonverbal communication, individuals can hone their skills in this area, resulting in improved communication outcomes and stronger interpersonal connections.

Beyond the realms of politics and business, nonverbal communication finds its significance in various other fields such as education, healthcare, and even technology. Each field requires its unique set of nonverbal cues, tailored to its specific context and audience.

Educators, for example, utilize nonverbal cues to establish a conducive learning environment and foster student engagement. An approachable posture, welcoming facial expressions, and attentive listening can create an atmosphere of trust and openness, encouraging students to participate and express their thoughts freely. Moreover, by varying their tone of voice and using gestures, educators can emphasize key points in their lessons, improving retention and comprehension among students.

In the healthcare sector, doctors and healthcare professionals rely heavily on nonverbal communication to convey empathy and establish trust with their patients. Patients often gauge their caregiver's empathy and attentiveness through their nonverbal cues. Therefore, maintaining eye contact, displaying a calm and patient demeanor, and using touch appropriately can reassure patients and make them feel understood and cared for.

As we delve into the realm of technology, the significance of nonverbal communication continues to grow. In this digital age, the nature of communication is evolving with the rise of video conferencing, virtual reality, and artificial intelligence. These technological advancements necessitate the effective use of nonverbal cues to compensate for the lack of physical proximity and maintain the richness of face-to-face interaction.

For example, in a video conferencing scenario, effective use of facial expressions, eye contact, and hand gestures can significantly improve the clarity of the message and establish a sense of engagement and connection with the audience. Similarly, in the realm of virtual reality, nonverbal cues are used to create more realistic and immersive experiences. Users can employ gestures and movements to interact with the virtual environment, providing a more engaging and intuitive form of communication.

Even artificial intelligence (AI) is being designed to understand and mimic human nonverbal cues. AI-powered chatbots and virtual assistants are being equipped with capabilities to understand and respond to users' emotions and intentions based on their tone of voice, speech patterns, and facial expressions. This incorporation of nonverbal cues in AI technology enhances user interaction and satisfaction, creating a more human-like and personalized experience.

While the importance of nonverbal communication is undeniable across various fields, it is equally crucial to remember its potential pitfalls. Misinterpretations of nonverbal cues can lead to misunderstanding and conflict. Hence, it is important to ensure that nonverbal cues align with verbal messages and the context of the communication. It is also essential to be sensitive to cultural differences, as nonverbal cues can vary significantly across different cultures.

So, nonverbal communication transcends the boundaries of spoken language, adding depth and nuance to our interactions. It finds its relevance in various domains, from politics and business to education, healthcare, and technology. As we move forward in this increasingly interconnected and digital world, mastering nonverbal communication will remain pivotal to effective communication, establishing rapport, and fostering meaningful connections.

Seductive Body Language in Management

Seductive body language in management represents a fascinating intersection between the realms of leadership, communication, and psychology. This unique form of nonverbal communication utilizes a series of conscious and subconscious cues to influence and engage individuals, leaving a lasting and positive impression. It's a delicate dance of gestures, postures, and expressions that, when deployed appropriately, can transform the dynamics of a workplace, setting the stage for enhanced interpersonal relationships, increased productivity, and heightened employee morale.

At the heart of this concept is the idea of attraction, but not in the romantic sense. Instead, it's about attracting attention, respect, and positive engagement from others. It's a magnetism that makes people want to listen, cooperate, and contribute. The idea is to create a positive aura that encourages open communication and fosters a healthy and productive work environment.

Leaders who master the art of seductive body language can create a strong presence that commands attention. This might involve maintaining confident postures, using expressive gestures to emphasize key points, and establishing eye contact to foster connection and trust. This physical embodiment of confidence and charisma can serve to inspire teams and promote a strong, unified work culture.

However, seductive body language in management is not just about the leader's presence or actions—it's equally about perceiving and responding to the nonverbal cues of team members. An effective leader understands the importance of 'listening' to the body language of their team, interpreting their emotions and attitudes, and adjusting their own nonverbal communication in response. By doing so, they can foster a supportive environment where everyone feels heard, valued, and motivated.

The nuances of seductive body language in management are manifold and the impacts, profound. The exploration of this concept underscores the fact that leadership extends beyond words. It's also about the subtle, yet powerful signals sent through body language. When harnessed effectively, these signals can enhance the art of leadership, fostering an environment of respect, understanding, and mutual growth.

Nevertheless, it's crucial to remember that body language should always be used ethically and responsibly. It should not be a tool for manipulation but rather, a means of fostering authenticity, trust, and meaningful connection in the workplace. Furthermore, cultural sensitivities must be considered, as nonverbal cues can carry different meanings across different cultures.

With a comprehensive understanding of seductive body language, managers can elevate their leadership skills, creating a more engaging and effective work environment that drives both individual and collective success.

The Power of Seductive Body Language

The effectiveness of seductive body language, when integrated seamlessly into a leader's repertoire, is truly transformative. It serves as a fundamental tool for persuasion and influence, navigating the landscape of human interactions with an air of assured charm. It's about gracefully commanding a room, not through domineering tactics, but rather through the unspoken appeal of confident, assured charisma that magnetizes attention and respect.

At the core of this powerful nonverbal communication is the concept of connection. It's the ability to non-verbally signal empathy and understanding, reaching out to others on an emotional and psychological level. The way a leader holds their posture, for instance, can project an image of openness and approachability that invites conversation and collaboration. A warm and authentic smile can instill a sense of comfort and camaraderie, enhancing team cohesion and boosting morale. Sustained, empathetic eye contact can foster trust and mutual respect, facilitating open and honest communication within the team.

Seductive body language is also a potent tool for shaping and enhancing the leader's personal brand. It provides an unspoken narrative about the leader's confidence, competence, and credibility. For instance, the confidence conveyed by an assertive yet relaxed stance, coupled with purposeful gestures, can instill a sense of assurance in the team, boosting their trust in the leader's abilities. This silent narrative enhances the leader's personal charisma, thereby augmenting their influence within the organization.

However, this power isn't just about exuding confidence and charisma; it's also about sensitivity and adaptability. Leaders who harness the power of seductive body language are also attuned to the nonverbal signals of their team members. They read and respond to these cues in a way that demonstrates understanding and empathy, thereby fostering a supportive and inclusive work environment. This two-way street of nonverbal communication allows for a deeper level of connection, fostering a sense of mutual trust and respect.

Additionally, the seductive power of body language extends beyond the immediate interactions within the workplace. It has lasting impacts that shape the overall work culture and climate. When leaders consistently exhibit positive, engaging body language, it sets a tone for the entire organization. It communicates expectations about the quality of interactions and the value of open, respectful communication, contributing to a more collaborative and effective work environment.

In essence, the power of seductive body language in management lies not just in its immediate impacts, but also in the lasting impressions it leaves. It shapes the perception of the leader, influences the dynamics of team interactions, and ultimately, sets the tone for the organization's culture. It's a silent orchestra conducted by the leader, producing harmonious work relationships that are vital for organizational success.

Key Elements of Seductive Body Language

Posture and Body Alignment

Delving deeper into the concept, posture and body alignment are more than just maintaining a straight back or preventing slouched shoulders; they're a fundamental aspect of the nonverbal communication toolkit that carries significant implications for leadership.

An upright posture is a universal symbol of self-assuredness and confidence. When a leader stands or sits tall, it naturally conveys a sense of strength and capability. It's as if they're metaphorically ready to take on any challenge, demonstrating their resilience and fortitude. This form of body language is quite powerful as it subconsciously communicates to others that the leader is competent and dependable.

Moreover, this physical manifestation of confidence can be an effective way to boost one's self-confidence internally. The act of positioning oneself confidently can, in a sense, trick the mind into feeling more confident. This phenomenon, often referred to as "embodied cognition," suggests that our mind-body connection is strong and that our body's actions can influence our mental states. Thus, maintaining an upright posture can be an effective strategy for enhancing one's self-assuredness in leadership situations.

On the other hand, the body alignment, specifically maintaining an open stance, is equally crucial in the art of seductive body language. An open stance refers to a posture where the body is oriented towards the other person, typically without any barriers like crossed arms or legs. It sends a clear message of receptiveness and approachability, indicating that the leader is open to ideas, feedback, and dialogue. It communicates a sense of respect and attentiveness to the team, fostering an atmosphere of collaboration and open communication.

Furthermore, body alignment also plays a crucial role in making connections and building rapport. Mirroring, a technique often used in interpersonal communication, involves subtly matching another person's body language. When leaders mirror their team members' body language, it can create a sense of harmony and mutual understanding, enhancing interpersonal connections.

However, posture and body alignment must be approached with a level of authenticity to effectively communicate the intended message. Overly rigid or exaggerated postures can come across as artificial or intimidating, potentially creating a barrier instead of fostering connection. It's about finding a balance where one's body language aligns with their natural demeanor and leadership style, enhancing their charismatic appeal without compromising their authenticity.

In essence, maintaining an upright posture and confident body alignment serves as a silent yet potent tool for leaders. It forms a vital part of seductive body language, enhancing the leader's charismatic appeal, and fostering a culture of openness and collaboration within the team. By mastering this art, leaders can significantly enhance their influence, build stronger relationships, and create a more engaging and inclusive work environment.

Eye Contact

Eye contact is a powerful tool in seductive body language. It is a fundamental aspect of nonverbal communication that can convey trust, connection, and engagement. The eyes are often referred to as the windows to the soul, as they reveal emotions, intentions, and authenticity. When used effectively, eye contact can create a magnetic presence, captivating the attention of others and establishing a deep connection.

The significance of eye contact in seductive body language lies in its ability to establish trust and build rapport. When a leader maintains direct eye contact with their team members, it signals that they are fully present and actively listening. It conveys a sense of genuine interest and respect, making individuals feel valued and acknowledged. This can create a safe and open environment where team members feel comfortable expressing their thoughts, concerns, and ideas.

Furthermore, eye contact fosters a sense of connection and emotional engagement. It allows leaders to establish a deeper level of understanding and empathy with their team members. Through sustained eye contact, leaders can convey compassion, support, and encouragement, which can enhance collaboration and foster a positive team dynamic.

However, it is important to note that there is a delicate balance when it comes to eye contact. Excessive or intense eye contact can become uncomfortable or intimidating, potentially undermining the desired effect of seductive body language. It is crucial for leaders to be mindful of cultural differences and individual preferences regarding eye contact. Some cultures may interpret prolonged eye contact as a sign of aggression or disrespect, while others may perceive it as a gesture of sincerity and trust. Leaders must adapt their eye contact to the cultural context and the comfort level of their team members.

Maintaining appropriate eye contact also involves gauging the dynamics of a conversation. In a one-on-one interaction, direct eye contact is crucial for establishing a personal connection and demonstrating undivided attention. It creates a sense of intimacy and engagement, conveying that the leader is fully present in the conversation. However, in group settings, leaders should distribute their eye contact evenly among participants, ensuring that everyone feels included and valued.

In addition to maintaining eye contact, leaders can utilize other nonverbal cues in conjunction with eye contact to enhance their seductive body language. Smiling while making eye contact can create a warm and inviting atmosphere, making others feel comfortable and at ease. Nodding in agreement or leaning slightly forward can show active listening and engagement, reinforcing the connection established through eye contact.

It is important to remember that eye contact alone is not enough to create a seductive presence as a leader. It should be combined with other elements of nonverbal communication, such as a confident posture, appropriate gestures, and vocal tone, to convey a consistent message. When all these components align harmoniously, leaders can exude a charismatic and influential presence that captivates their team and inspires them to perform at their best.

In conclusion, eye contact is a powerful tool in seductive body language. It has the ability to establish trust, build rapport, and foster emotional engagement. When used appropriately, eye contact can create a deep connection between leaders and their team members. However, it is essential for leaders to be mindful of cultural differences and individual preferences regarding eye contact. By combining eye contact with other nonverbal cues, leaders can enhance their seductive body language and create a magnetic presence that inspires and influences others.

Facial Expressions

Facial expressions play a crucial role in seductive body language as they are a powerful means of conveying emotions, intentions, and attitudes. Among the various facial expressions, a warm and inviting smile holds particular significance in creating a positive and welcoming atmosphere. A genuine smile not only signals approachability but also has the power to instantly uplift the mood of others.

When a leader greets their team members with a warm smile, it communicates a sense of openness and friendliness. This simple gesture can break down barriers and create a positive first impression, making individuals feel comfortable and valued. A smile has the ability to put others at ease, establishing a welcoming atmosphere where collaboration and engagement thrive. Moreover, smiling releases endorphins, which are neurotransmitters that contribute to feelings of happiness and well-being. By evoking positive emotions, a smile can significantly influence the mood and engagement of others, fostering a conducive environment for productive interactions.

Apart from smiling, leaders can employ subtle facial expressions to convey empathy, understanding, and encouragement. Nonverbal cues such as nodding in agreement or raising an eyebrow to show curiosity can enhance active listening and foster meaningful connections. When a leader nods in agreement, it signals that they are attentively listening and validating the thoughts and ideas being expressed.

This simple act of affirmation creates a sense of understanding and encourages open dialogue. Similarly, raising an eyebrow can demonstrate curiosity and genuine interest in what others have to say, encouraging further exploration of their perspectives. These micro-expressions can build trust and rapport, contributing to a seductive body language that captivates and engages others.

It is important to note that facial expressions should be authentic and congruent with the underlying emotions. Leaders should aim for genuine expressions that reflect their true intentions and feelings. Authenticity is key in building trust and establishing a seductive presence. Forced or insincere facial expressions can be easily detected and may hinder effective communication and connection.

In addition to facial expressions, leaders can utilize other facial cues to enhance their seductive body language. Maintaining appropriate eye contact while smiling or expressing empathy further amplifies the impact of facial expressions. Direct eye contact during a warm smile intensifies its effect, creating a more personal and engaging connection. Likewise, combining nodding with eye contact conveys active listening and genuine understanding, fostering a deeper level of connection and empathy. These nonverbal cues work in harmony to establish a seductive presence that captures the attention and trust of others.

Practicing and developing awareness of facial expressions can help leaders enhance their seductive body language. Self-reflection and observation of one's own facial expressions in different situations can provide valuable insights into how they are perceived by others. Seeking feedback from trusted colleagues or coaches can also aid in refining facial expressions and ensuring their alignment with the intended message.

In summary, facial expressions play a crucial role in seductive body language. A warm and inviting smile can instantly create a positive and welcoming atmosphere, influencing the mood and engagement of others. Authenticity in facial expressions is vital for establishing trust and building rapport. Leaders can further enhance their seductive body language by using subtle facial expressions, such as nodding and raising an eyebrow, to convey empathy, understanding, and encouragement.

When combined with other nonverbal cues, such as eye contact, facial expressions contribute to a cohesive and impactful communication style that captivates and inspires others.

Gestures and Hand Movements

The strategic use of gestures and hand movements is an essential aspect of seductive body language in management. When employed effectively, these nonverbal cues can enhance communication, emphasize key points, and create visual interest during presentations or discussions. Gestures can help leaders convey confidence, engage their audience, and make their presentations more memorable. However, it is important for leaders to be mindful of their gestures, ensuring they are natural, purposeful, and complementary to their verbal message.

Smooth and purposeful gestures can add emphasis and reinforce the intended message. For example, using an open palm to emphasize a point or making a sweeping motion with the hands to illustrate a concept can captivate the audience's attention and make the information more engaging. Leaders can strategically utilize gestures to guide the flow of conversation, indicating transitions between ideas or segments. These purposeful movements create visual interest, capturing the audience's attention and maintaining their engagement throughout the presentation.

It is important for leaders to be mindful of the frequency and intensity of their gestures. Avoiding overly repetitive or exaggerated movements is crucial, as it can distract from the intended message and undermine the effectiveness of seductive body language. A balanced approach is key, ensuring that gestures enhance the verbal message without overpowering it. Leaders should observe their own gestures and seek feedback from others to identify any distracting or repetitive movements that may detract from the overall impact.

The naturalness of gestures is also essential. Leaders should strive for gestures that feel authentic and aligned with their personal style and message. Forced or unnatural movements can create a sense of inauthenticity and disconnect with the audience. Practicing and refining gestures in a way that feels comfortable and genuine helps leaders maintain a confident and charismatic presence.

In addition to hand movements, leaders can consider the use of other nonverbal cues in conjunction with gestures to enhance their seductive body language. Facial expressions, eye contact, and vocal variations can work in harmony with hand movements, creating a cohesive and engaging communication style. For example, maintaining eye contact while using a gesture can strengthen its impact and foster a stronger connection with the audience. Similarly, aligning facial expressions with gestures can convey emotions, enthusiasm, and authenticity, further enhancing the overall impact of seductive body language.

Awareness of cultural differences is crucial when utilizing gestures in a diverse environment. Gestures can vary in meaning across cultures, and what may be appropriate or effective in one culture may not be the same in another. Leaders should be sensitive to these differences and adapt their gestures accordingly, ensuring that they are respectful and well-received by their audience.

In conclusion, the strategic use of gestures and hand movements can greatly enhance seductive body language in management. Smooth and purposeful gestures add emphasis, create visual interest, and engage the audience during presentations or discussions. Leaders should be mindful of the naturalness, frequency, and intensity of their gestures to ensure they are complementary to their verbal message. By combining gestures with other nonverbal cues, such as facial expressions and eye contact, leaders can create a cohesive and impactful communication style that captivates their audience, conveys confidence, and makes their presentations more memorable.

Proxemics

The concept of proxemics, or the study and interpretation of human use of space, introduces a facet of communication that often goes unacknowledged in traditional discourses of management. Its implications seep into the layers of interpersonal communication, nonverbal cues, and implicit messages conveyed through body language, all contributing to the collective perception of leadership. Proxemics doesn't only imply spatial relation but extends into the domain of respect for personal boundaries, empathy, cultural sensitivity, and creating a work environment where individuals feel both comfortable and motivated.

Effective leaders, ones who have imbibed the essence of people management, demonstrate their acumen by acknowledging the importance of appropriate proxemics. These leaders don't merely dictate or delegate, but interact, engage, and co-create.

Their use of physical space is considerate, well-measured, and contextually appropriate. Leaders are aware that the way they navigate the space around their team members can directly impact how comfortable, respected, and valued these individuals feel.

Cultural norms and individual preferences inform the parameters within which leaders operate when using physical space during interactions. Every culture perceives and utilizes physical space differently. Some cultures may consider closer proximity as a symbol of trust and warmth, while others might perceive the same as an infringement of personal boundaries. A leader who showcases cultural sensitivity by adapting to these varied norms can foster an environment of mutual respect, ultimately driving higher productivity and job satisfaction among diverse teams.

Personal preferences and comfort regarding physical space are as crucial as cultural norms. Every individual comes with unique thresholds and preferences when it comes to personal space, something a leader should be cognizant of. An attuned leader can pick up on cues from their team members, adjusting their proximity in a manner that respects individual comfort levels. This not only cultivates a feeling of being valued but also helps establish trust, an essential ingredient for any successful team.

Striking a balance in the use of physical space is an art that leaders must master to create an optimal work environment. An overly distant leader may project an image of disinterest, approachability, or detachment, thereby affecting the rapport with team members. This can impede effective communication and collaboration, crucial elements of a thriving work ecosystem.

Conversely, invading personal space can cause discomfort, potentially breaching trust and creating an environment of unease. A leader must therefore adeptly maintain a balance, ensuring accessibility without overstepping personal boundaries.

By mastering the subtle art of proxemics, leaders can craft an atmosphere that promotes trust, collaboration, and innovation. This involves adapting their use of space according to cultural norms and individual preferences, displaying a high degree of respect and consideration.

With this careful balance, leaders can create a supportive environment where team members feel comfortable expressing their thoughts and ideas, fostering a culture of open communication, and driving the collective success of the team. This heightened awareness of proxemics allows leaders to tap into a deeper level of interpersonal connection, adding a new dimension to their leadership toolkit, and transforming the way their team interacts, collaborates, and performs.

Practical insights for leaders in mastering proxemics include:

- *Cultural Sensitivity*:
  Cultural sensitivity is an integral element in the mastery of proxemics within leadership. It requires leaders to invest time and effort in understanding the cultural norms and expectations of their team members.
  Each culture has its own unique perspectives and practices regarding personal space and physical proximity during interactions. By proactively seeking to comprehend these cultural nuances, leaders demonstrate a commitment to inclusivity and respect for diversity.
  Cross-cultural training and education can be valuable tools for leaders in

gaining insights into appropriate proxemics in diverse environments. Such training helps leaders develop a broader understanding of cultural differences and the ways in which they shape individuals' perceptions of personal space. It equips leaders with knowledge about the cultural context and preferences of their team members, enabling them to adapt their behavior and proximity accordingly.

By taking the initiative to learn about different cultural perspectives on personal space, leaders demonstrate their respect for and appreciation of diversity. This initiative sends a powerful message that they value the unique backgrounds and experiences of their team members. It creates an environment where individuals from various cultural backgrounds feel included, respected, and valued for who they are.

Cultural sensitivity allows leaders to adapt their behavior and proximity in a way that aligns with the cultural preferences of their team members. Leaders who are culturally sensitive understand that what may be considered acceptable personal space in one culture may not hold true in another. They adapt their approach to ensure that their actions and proximity are in line with the cultural expectations and comfort levels of their team members.

By demonstrating cultural sensitivity, leaders create an environment where individuals from diverse backgrounds feel valued and included. This fosters a sense of belonging, psychological safety, and trust within the team. When team members feel that their cultural backgrounds and personal space preferences are respected, they are more likely to feel comfortable expressing themselves, sharing ideas, and engaging in open and honest communication.

Effective communication and collaboration are nurtured in an environment where cultural sensitivity is valued. When leaders show a genuine interest in understanding and adapting to different cultural perspectives on personal space, they create a foundation for effective cross-cultural communication. Team members are more likely to feel understood, respected, and heard, which in turn enhances their willingness to engage and collaborate with others.

Cultural sensitivity also facilitates the creation of a diverse and inclusive work culture. By valuing and embracing cultural differences, leaders promote an environment that celebrates diversity and allows team members to bring their authentic selves to work. This leads to a rich exchange of ideas, perspectives, and experiences, which can ultimately drive innovation and creativity within the team.

- *Observation and Adaptation*:

Observation and adaptation are crucial skills for leaders seeking to master proxemics in their leadership approach. Leaders should actively observe the body language and nonverbal cues of their team members during interactions, as these cues can provide valuable information about their comfort levels and preferred physical distance.

By attentively observing the body language of team members, leaders can gain insights into their comfort levels in terms of physical proximity. They can observe whether individuals lean in or lean back during conversations, whether they maintain direct eye contact, or if they exhibit signs of discomfort or tension. These subtle cues can provide important clues about how individuals perceive and respond to their physical space during interactions.

Adaptation is the next critical step for leaders in fostering an environment where individuals feel respected and at ease. Leaders who adapt their proximity according to the nonverbal cues they observe can create a sense of comfort and respect for personal boundaries. For instance, if a team member appears to lean in or exhibit engagement cues, the leader can choose to move closer, demonstrating attentiveness and creating a connection. Conversely, if a team member displays signs of discomfort or prefers more personal space, the leader can maintain a respectful distance.

By adapting their proximity accordingly, leaders send a message of respect and consideration to their team members. This approach acknowledges that personal space preferences can vary among individuals and respects their boundaries. It fosters an environment where individuals feel valued and comfortable during interactions, promoting open communication and trust.

Observation and adaptation go beyond physical proximity alone. Leaders should also pay attention to other nonverbal cues, such as facial expressions, body posture, and gestures. These cues can provide insights into the emotional state and receptiveness of team members. For example, a team member displaying closed body language or signs of stress may indicate a need for more personal space and a cautious approach.

Leaders who observe and adapt their proximity demonstrate their ability to empathize and connect with their team members on a deeper level. They show that they are attuned to the needs and comfort of others, creating an environment where individuals feel valued and understood. This fosters trust, encourages open communication, and enhances the overall dynamics and productivity of the team.

It is important for leaders to note that observation and adaptation should be done with sensitivity and awareness. They should be mindful of individual differences and cultural variations in personal space preferences. Leaders should be adaptable and flexible in their approach, taking into account the diverse backgrounds and comfort levels of their team members.

- *Open Communication*:
  Open communication is a fundamental aspect of mastering proxemics in leadership. By encouraging open dialogue and feedback regarding personal space preferences, leaders can create a culture of trust and respect within their teams. This open communication allows team members to feel comfortable expressing their needs and preferences, enabling them to establish mutually beneficial proxemics.

  Creating an environment where team members feel safe and supported in sharing their personal space preferences is essential. Leaders can initiate conversations and discussions about personal space in team meetings or one-on-one interactions. By addressing the topic openly, leaders demonstrate their willingness to listen and accommodate individual needs.

Encouraging open dialogue about personal space preferences allows team members to express their comfort levels and boundaries without fear of judgment or repercussion. It provides an opportunity for individuals to voice their concerns, preferences, and any adjustments they may require to feel more comfortable during interactions. This open communication fosters trust and respect within the team, as team members know their opinions and preferences are valued and respected.

Leaders should create a safe and non-judgmental space for team members to share their personal space preferences. They can actively listen to their team members' concerns and provide support and understanding. This open communication creates an atmosphere where individuals feel empowered to establish mutually beneficial proxemics that respect their comfort levels and boundaries.

By encouraging open communication about personal space preferences, leaders can also gain valuable insights into the unique needs and comfort levels of their team members. This knowledge allows leaders to tailor their approach and adapt their proximity to align with the preferences of individual team members. It shows a genuine commitment to creating an inclusive and comfortable work environment.

Furthermore, open communication about personal space preferences fosters a culture of respect and consideration within the team. It encourages team members to be mindful of each other's boundaries and adapt their behavior accordingly. This leads to increased empathy, understanding, and collaboration within the team.

It is important for leaders to create an ongoing dialogue around personal space preferences rather than treating it as a one-time conversation. Team dynamics, individual preferences, and comfort levels may evolve over time. Leaders should regularly check in with team members and provide opportunities for open communication and feedback regarding personal space.

- *<u>Mindful Body Language</u>*:

    Mindful body language is a crucial aspect of mastering proxemics in leadership. Leaders should be aware of their own body language during interactions and consciously make necessary adjustments to respect personal space. By being mindful of their physical proximity, leaders can enhance their effectiveness as communicators and influencers.

Being aware of one's body language allows leaders to create a positive and respectful environment. It involves paying attention to the distance between themselves and others, as well as their own gestures, facial expressions, and posture. Leaders who are mindful of their body language project an image of approachability, authenticity, and respect.

One aspect of mindful body language is being conscious of personal proximity. Leaders should be aware of the appropriate physical distance that makes team members feel comfortable during interactions. This may vary depending on cultural norms and individual preferences. By maintaining an appropriate distance, leaders show respect for personal boundaries and create a sense of comfort for team members.

Mindful body language also involves making necessary adjustments to adapt to different situations and individuals. For example, in a one-on-one conversation, leaders may choose to lean in slightly to demonstrate active listening and engagement. In a group setting, leaders may adjust their proximity to ensure that everyone feels included and engaged in the conversation.

Another aspect of mindful body language is being aware of nonverbal cues and gestures. Leaders should pay attention to their own body language to ensure that it aligns with their intended message. This includes maintaining open and relaxed posture, making eye contact, and using appropriate hand gestures. These nonverbal cues can enhance the clarity and impact of their communication, making it more effective and influential.

By being mindful of their body language, leaders create an environment where team members feel respected and valued. When leaders are aware of their physical proximity and make necessary adjustments, they demonstrate their attentiveness and consideration for others. This fosters trust, collaboration, and open communication within the team.

Moreover, mindful body language enhances leaders' ability to influence and inspire others. When leaders are conscious of their own nonverbal cues, they can effectively convey their messages and engage their team members. They can create a positive and receptive atmosphere that encourages active participation and collaboration.

Leaders who are mindful of their body language also set a positive example for their team members. They demonstrate the importance of nonverbal communication and encourage others to be mindful of their own body language. This promotes a culture of open and effective communication within the team.

- Tone of Voice and Vocal Inflection

Tone of voice and vocal inflection are fundamental aspects of communication that greatly influence how our messages are perceived and understood. While body language primarily focuses on nonverbal cues, the way we speak carries a wealth of information and plays a crucial role in conveying emotions, attitudes, and intentions.

The tone of voice encompasses the quality, character, and emotional undertones of our voice. It serves as an auditory companion to our words, adding depth and nuance to our communication. When leaders strive to cultivate a confident and expressive tone, they project authority, charisma, and enthusiasm, thereby capturing the attention and respect of their audience. A powerful and well-modulated voice can be persuasive, inspiring, and even seductive, enabling leaders to effectively influence and motivate others.

Expressiveness is another key element of tone of voice. By skillfully employing variations in pitch, volume, and pace, individuals can convey a wide range of emotions and effectively emphasize key points. An expressive voice can evoke interest, excitement, or empathy, creating a dynamic and engaging experience for listeners.

Conversely, a monotonous or flat delivery can dull the impact of our message and disengage our audience. By harnessing the power of vocal inflection, leaders can breathe life into their words, making them more memorable and impactful.

Strategic pauses also contribute to effective vocal communication. Well-placed pauses can lend weight and significance to specific words or ideas, allowing the audience to absorb and reflect upon them. Pauses can create anticipation, build suspense, or provide a moment for listeners to process information. Skillful use of pauses enables leaders to control the rhythm and flow of their speech, making it easier for the audience to understand and engage with their ideas.

Furthermore, the volume and pace at which we speak significantly impact our communication. Speaking too softly can make it difficult for listeners to hear and comprehend our message, while speaking too loudly can overwhelm or intimidate them. Striking the right balance ensures that our words are clearly conveyed and received.

Similarly, pacing plays a vital role in effective communication. Speaking too quickly can leave listeners struggling to keep up, while speaking too slowly may lead to disengagement. Leaders should aim for a moderate pace that allows for clarity and comprehension while keeping the audience engaged and attentive.

It is essential to consider the context and audience when determining the appropriate tone of voice and vocal inflection. Different situations call for different approaches. For instance, a persuasive speech may require more emphasis and vocal variety to captivate and retain the attention of the audience.

On the other hand, delivering bad news or providing comfort may call for a calm and soothing tone. Adapting our tone and inflection to suit the specific circumstances enhances the effectiveness of communication, ensuring that the intended message is accurately conveyed and received.

In summary, tone of voice and vocal inflection are integral to effective communication. A confident and expressive tone, coupled with appropriate pauses and variations in pitch, can captivate listeners and make our message more engaging. Leaders should be mindful of their volume and pace to ensure clarity and comprehension, thereby facilitating effective communication. By harnessing the power of tone of voice and vocal inflection, individuals can become more persuasive, charismatic, and influential communicators. They can foster stronger connections with others, convey their messages with clarity and authority, and ultimately make a lasting impact.

Practical Insights for Leaders

Self-Awareness: Developing self-awareness is the first step toward mastering seductive body language. Leaders should take time to observe their own body language, identifying areas for improvement and reflecting on the impact their nonverbal cues may have on others. Seeking feedback from trusted colleagues or engaging in video self-analysis can provide valuable insights for personal growth.

Practice and Rehearse: Like any skill, seductive body language requires practice. Leaders can benefit from rehearsing presentations or important conversations, paying attention to their body language and making necessary adjustments. Recording and reviewing practice sessions can help identify areas for improvement and refine nonverbal cues.

Cultural Sensitivity: Cultural norms and expectations regarding body language may vary across regions and organizations. Leaders should be sensitive to these differences and adapt their nonverbal cues accordingly. Cross-cultural training and awareness can help leaders navigate diverse environments with cultural sensitivity and respect.

Authenticity: While it is important to master seductive body language, leaders should also prioritize authenticity. Nonverbal cues should align with their true personality and values, as inauthentic body language can create a sense of dissonance and distrust. Leaders who strike a balance between employing seductive body language techniques and remaining authentic can effectively engage their team and build lasting connections.

Continuous Improvement: Seductive body language is an ongoing journey of growth and refinement. Leaders should seek opportunities to expand their knowledge and skills in nonverbal communication. Attending workshops, reading relevant books or articles, and observing successful communicators can provide valuable insights and inspire continuous improvement.

By harnessing the power of seductive body language, leaders can create an atmosphere of charisma, influence, and trust within their teams. Mastering the key elements of seductive body language, such as posture, eye contact, facial expressions, gestures, proxemics, tone of voice, and vocal inflection, empowers leaders to effectively communicate their messages, inspire their teams, and cultivate positive relationships.

Through self-awareness, practice, cultural sensitivity, authenticity, and a commitment to continuous improvement, leaders can unlock the full potential of seductive body language in their management approach.

So, seductive body language holds significant potential for leaders in the management realm. The deliberate and skillful use of nonverbal cues can captivate attention, inspire trust, and foster meaningful connections with team members.

By understanding the key elements of seductive body language and incorporating practical insights, leaders can enhance their communication, influence, and overall effectiveness in the workplace. Mastering seductive body language is a continuous journey of self-awareness, practice, and refinement, ultimately leading to more engaging and impactful leadership.

Using Seductive Voice and Tone

While there's no denying the captivating allure of a seductive voice, mastering this skill requires a deep understanding of its numerous elements and their potential effects. The use of voice as a means of seduction transcends simple dialogue - it's a holistic tool designed to sway, persuade, and forge connections.

A seductive voice and tone thrive on their ability to trigger emotional responses. Speaking in a smooth, harmonious manner resonates with listeners on a deeply visceral level. This emotional engagement can open doors to persuasive conversations, especially in fields such as sales and marketing, where the aim is to generate an appealing image of a product or service.

Vocal inflection, or the modulation of one's voice, is another critical piece of the seductive voice puzzle. By strategically adjusting pitch, rhythm, and stress on certain words, one can control the narrative, making conversations feel more animated and engaging. A well-timed vocal inflection can pique curiosity, spark excitement, and create an overall dynamic communication experience.

The volume and pace of speech, too, play integral roles in seductive voice communication. Speaking softly can invite intimacy, pulling the listener in, urging them to concentrate on the speaker's words. On the other hand, a sudden increase in volume can punctuate phrases, offering emotional depth to specific parts of the conversation. Slow speech pace can reinforce key points, ensuring the listener absorbs the crux of the message.

Despite the potential benefits, employing a seductive voice and tone demands careful consideration and ethical responsibility. Misusing these techniques can lead to damaging manipulation and exploitation, which not only harm relationships and reputations but also breach moral boundaries.

Sensitivity to cultural and personal interpretations of seductive communication is also paramount. Individuals and societies possess diverse perceptions about what's considered seductive or appealing, underscoring the need to navigate these waters with empathy and understanding. Violating personal comfort zones or crossing cultural boundaries can tarnish communication and lead to discomfort or miscommunication.

Furthermore, it's crucial to discern when it's appropriate to use a seductive voice and tone. Not all contexts are suitable for this form of communication - there are environments, particularly professional ones, where a seductive tone might be deemed unprofessional or inappropriate. The ability to adapt one's communication style to the demands of a situation is a valuable skill that bolsters respectful and effective interaction.

Utilizing a seductive voice and tone can indeed be a powerful communication technique, particularly when the aim is to inspire desire or attraction. However, this art requires ethical usage, careful calibration to cultural and personal boundaries, and the ability to adapt to context. When employed with these considerations in mind, a seductive voice and tone can elevate the art of communication, leading to meaningful, impactful exchanges.

When approaching the use of seductive voice and tone, it's important to bear in mind that the primary aim isn't to manipulate or control, but to foster a genuine connection with the listener. By imbuing their words with emotion, warmth, and sincerity, communicators can ensure their messages resonate on a more personal and emotional level. This can lead to deeper and more nuanced relationships, enabling a more profound understanding between individuals.

Practicing vocal modulation is a significant step towards mastering seductive communication. This includes understanding how to vary the pitch and tone to suit the emotional content of the message. High pitches can convey excitement or urgency, while lower tones might suggest seriousness or authority. Incorporating these variations in voice can add a layer of expressiveness and personal touch to communication, making it more engaging and compelling for the listener.

Rhythm and pace also play a part in making a voice sound more seductive. Delivering words at a slower pace allows the listener time to absorb the information, adding an air of suspense or importance. On the other hand, quickening the speech tempo can create an impression of excitement or eagerness. Effectively managing these dynamics can make the conversation more captivating, keeping the listener hooked on every word.

However, while the seductive voice is a powerful tool, it's crucial to remember that its effects can be significantly enhanced when coupled with congruent body language. The non-verbal cues should match the tone and content of the spoken words. For example, maintaining eye contact while speaking in a seductive tone can create a sense of intimacy and demonstrate sincerity. Similarly, open body language can suggest honesty and vulnerability, enhancing the perception of authenticity.

Also, understanding the listener's responses and adapting the communication style accordingly is fundamental for effective seductive communication. This involves being perceptive of the listener's reactions, both verbal and nonverbal, and adjusting the communication style to suit their comfort level and receptiveness. Such responsiveness demonstrates empathy and respect, leading to more positive communication outcomes.

In the end, the essence of seductive communication lies in its capacity to create a bridge of understanding between individuals, facilitating the transmission of ideas and emotions in a captivating manner. The aim is not just to speak, but to engage, not only to inform but to connect. In the right hands, and used with respect and responsibility, seductive voice and tone can transform the way we interact, turning ordinary conversations into meaningful exchanges, filled with understanding and shared sentiments.

So, whether you are a leader seeking to inspire a team, a salesperson aiming to connect with a client, or simply an individual striving for richer personal relationships, mastering the art of seductive communication can significantly enhance your interpersonal skills and the quality of your interactions. Remember, the aim is not just to communicate, but to resonate, to evoke, and most importantly, to connect.

The Art of Persuasion

The art of persuasion is a multifaceted skill that has been studied and honed throughout history. It is the ability to influence and convince others to adopt a specific viewpoint, take particular actions, or change their behavior. Persuasion is not about manipulation or coercion, but rather about presenting compelling arguments, appealing to emotions, and building trust and rapport with the audience. It requires a combination of effective communication techniques, logical reasoning, and an understanding of human psychology.

Effective communication is a fundamental element of persuasion. Persuasive communicators know how to convey their ideas clearly and concisely in a way that resonates with the target audience. They choose their words carefully, considering the emotional impact and desired outcome. They adapt their communication style to match the preferences and needs of the audience, whether it be through storytelling, using vivid imagery, or presenting concrete examples. By tailoring their message to the audience, persuasive communicators increase the likelihood of capturing attention and engaging listeners.

Emotional appeal is a powerful tool in persuasion. People are often driven by their emotions, and appealing to these emotions can be a persuasive strategy. Understanding the values, desires, and fears of the audience allows a persuasive communicator to craft messages that elicit emotional responses, creating a connection and resonance with the listeners. Whether it is tapping into a sense of belonging, appealing to compassion, or evoking a desire for personal gain, emotional appeal can significantly influence decision-making. By leveraging emotions effectively, persuasive communicators can sway opinions and inspire action.

Logical reasoning is another critical component of persuasion. Presenting a well-structured and logical argument provides a solid foundation for convincing others. This involves providing evidence, facts, and examples to support the claims being made. Persuasive communicators anticipate counterarguments and address them effectively, strengthening their position and minimizing potential objections. They rely on data, expert opinions, and credible sources to bolster their arguments and increase the credibility of their message. By using logical reasoning, persuasive communicators appeal to the intellect of the audience, enhancing the persuasiveness of their message.

Building trust and rapport is essential in the art of persuasion. People are more likely to be persuaded by those they trust and respect. Establishing credibility is crucial, and this can be achieved through expertise, personal experiences, or endorsements from trusted sources. Persuasive communicators actively listen to the concerns and perspectives of their audience, showing empathy and understanding. By building a genuine connection and demonstrating that they have the audience's best interests at heart, they foster trust, making their arguments more persuasive. Trust allows the audience to be more receptive to the communicator's message and increases the likelihood of agreement or action.

Adaptability is another key aspect of persuasion. Different individuals have different preferences, communication styles, and decision-making processes. A persuasive communicator recognizes this and adapts their approach accordingly. They tailor their arguments to resonate with the specific needs and values of the audience. By understanding the audience's motivations and perspectives, they can present their message in a way that is most likely to be persuasive and compelling. This adaptability allows persuasive communicators to connect with diverse audiences and increase the effectiveness of their persuasion efforts.

Timing and context also play a significant role in persuasion. Knowing when and where to present a persuasive message can greatly impact its effectiveness. A persuasive communicator chooses the opportune moment to engage with their audience, ensuring that they are receptive and open to considering new ideas.

They also take into account the cultural and social context, adapting their message to align with the prevailing norms and values of the audience. By considering timing and context, persuasive communicators maximize the impact of their message and increase the likelihood of successful persuasion and logical reasoning, trust-building, adaptability, and consideration of timing and context. Persuasive communicators possess the ability to influence and convince others by presenting compelling arguments, appealing to emotions, and establishing credibility and rapport. By mastering the art of persuasion, individuals can become more influential, empowering them to drive change, build relationships, and achieve their goals.

Timing and context are critical elements in the art of persuasion. Knowing when and where to deliver a persuasive message can significantly impact its effectiveness. A persuasive communicator carefully selects the opportune moment to engage with their audience, ensuring that they are receptive and open to considering new ideas. By identifying the right timing, communicators can capitalize on the audience's receptiveness, maximizing the chances of successful persuasion.

In addition to timing, considering the context in which the message is delivered is essential. Persuasive communicators take into account the cultural and social context, adapting their message to align with the prevailing norms, values, and beliefs of the audience. By understanding the cultural nuances and sensitivities, communicators can tailor their message to resonate with the audience on a deeper level. This cultural adaptability enhances the persuasiveness of the message and increases the likelihood of acceptance.

Furthermore, effective persuasion requires the ability to build trust and rapport with the audience. People are more likely to be persuaded by someone they trust and respect. Establishing credibility is crucial in gaining the audience's confidence.

Persuasive communicators achieve this by showcasing their expertise, sharing personal experiences, or leveraging endorsements from trusted sources. Building trust also involves active listening, empathy, and understanding. By genuinely engaging with the audience, communicators create a connection that fosters trust, making their arguments more persuasive.

Adaptability is a key attribute of persuasive communicators. Different individuals have distinct preferences, communication styles, and decision-making processes. Recognizing this, persuasive communicators adapt their approach to resonate with the specific needs and values of the audience. They tailor their arguments, language, and delivery to effectively communicate with different individuals or groups. This adaptability ensures that the message is received in a manner that is most persuasive and impactful, increasing the chances of influencing the audience's thoughts and actions.

Finally, logical reasoning serves as a foundation for persuasive arguments. Presenting a well-structured and logical argument provides the audience with a clear and rational basis for accepting the proposed viewpoint. Persuasive communicators support their claims with evidence, facts, and examples. They anticipate counterarguments and address them effectively, further strengthening their position. By relying on logical reasoning, persuasive communicators appeal to the intellect of the audience, enhancing the persuasiveness of their message.

The art of persuasion involves a combination of effective communication, emotional appeal, logical reasoning, trust-building, adaptability, and consideration of timing and context. Persuasive communicators possess the ability to influence and convince others by presenting compelling arguments, appealing to emotions, and establishing credibility and rapport. By mastering the art of persuasion, individuals can become more influential and persuasive in their communication efforts. This empowers them to drive change, build relationships, and achieve their goals effectively

Persuasion Strategies Based on Attraction

In the vast spectrum of human communication, persuasion stands out as an integral component. It is the process of guiding people towards the adoption of an idea, attitude, or action by rational or symbolic means. Certain persuasion strategies are primarily based on attraction, which denotes the pull or allure that one person feels towards another, primarily due to their qualities or traits that are considered desirable or appealing.

Attraction-based persuasion strategies essentially use the strength of personal appeal and charm to persuade others. This often involves creating a connection or establishing rapport with the individual or group you are trying to influence. The foundation of this approach lies in the fact that we are more likely to be persuaded by individuals we find attractive, trustworthy, and likable.

Underpinning the power of attraction in persuasion is the principle of affinity. Humans are naturally drawn to those they feel connected with or attracted to, whether on a personal or professional level. This affinity can be rooted in a multitude of factors, from shared interests, values, or experiences to a magnetic personality or charismatic aura.

The strategy of using attraction in persuasion is not confined to physical appeal. It extends to intellectual and emotional attraction as well. A persuasive individual may utilize their wit, knowledge, empathy, or storytelling ability to draw others in, facilitating a stronger connection and enhancing their influence.

Techniques involved in attraction-based persuasion can vary widely but are always grounded in the goal of enhancing one's appeal to the target audience. For instance, demonstrating empathy and understanding, expressing genuine interest in the other person, maintaining positive body language, and building rapport through shared experiences or interests are common techniques that enhance attractiveness and, consequently, persuasive potential.

Another critical aspect of attraction-based persuasion is emotional engagement. Emotions can significantly impact decision-making processes. Therefore, persuasion strategies that evoke emotions—such as storytelling, the use of vivid language or imagery, and appeals to shared values or experiences—can be particularly powerful. By sparking emotions in their audience, persuasive communicators can enhance their attractiveness and increase their influence.

Despite the potential effectiveness of attraction-based persuasion strategies, it's crucial to maintain an ethical stance. Persuasion should not veer into manipulation, and attractiveness should never be used to deceive or exploit. Respect for the autonomy and dignity of others is paramount.

In summary, attraction-based persuasion strategies provide a unique approach to influence others, capitalizing on the power of personal appeal and emotional connection. These strategies, rooted in the principles of likability, rapport, and emotional engagement, offer a compelling way to enhance one's persuasive influence. But, as with all forms of persuasion, they should be employed with a keen awareness of ethical implications and a fundamental respect for the integrity of others.

Establishing Rapport and Likability:

The foundation of attraction-based persuasion lies in building rapport and likability. People are naturally drawn to those they find friendly, approachable, and relatable. Effective communicators utilize techniques to establish rapport and create a positive connection with their audience. These techniques include:

a) *Mirroring body language*: By subtly matching and mirroring the nonverbal cues and gestures of their audience, communicators build a sense of familiarity and trust. Mirroring conveys a sense of shared understanding and can help establish rapport.

b) *Active listening*: Showing genuine interest in the concerns and perspectives of others fosters a sense of being heard and understood. Active listening involves attentively focusing on the speaker, maintaining eye contact, and responding empathetically. This approach deepens connections and strengthens rapport.

c) *Authenticity and relatability*: Communicators who exhibit authenticity and share personal experiences that resonate with their audience's challenges, aspirations, or values can create a sense of shared experiences. This relatability fosters likability and strengthens the persuasive impact of the message.

Emotional Appeal:

Emotions play a significant role in decision-making processes, and persuasive communicators leverage this by appealing to the emotions of their audience. By crafting messages that elicit emotional responses, communicators create a powerful connection that enhances their persuasive influence. Key techniques for emotional appeal include:

a) *Storytelling*: Engaging narratives that evoke emotion can captivate audiences and elicit empathy or identification. Stories have a unique ability to tap into the human experience and create a memorable, emotional impact that influences attitudes and behaviors.

b) *Creating a sense of shared values and aspirations*: Persuasive communicators align their message with the values, aspirations, and desires of their audience. By emphasizing how adopting their viewpoint or taking specific action aligns with the audience's core values and helps them achieve their aspirations, communicators create an emotional connection that enhances persuasion.

c) *Evoking positive and negative emotions*: By strategically triggering positive emotions like joy, hope, or excitement, communicators can create a sense of enthusiasm and motivation. Alternatively, invoking negative emotions such as fear or anger can highlight potential risks or consequences of inaction, increasing the urgency to act. Balancing the use of positive and negative emotions is crucial for ethical and effective persuasion.

Social Proof and Authority:

The principle of social proof suggests that people are more likely to be persuaded when they perceive others, especially those they respect or admire, as endorsing a particular viewpoint or action. Communicators can leverage social proof and authority to enhance their persuasive influence. Key strategies include:

> a) *Testimonials and endorsements*: Sharing testimonials from satisfied customers or influential individuals who support the communicator's message can significantly impact persuasiveness. When individuals see others expressing approval or satisfaction, they are more inclined to follow suit.

> b) *Expert opinions and credible sources*: By incorporating expert opinions, statistics, or data from reputable sources, communicators bolster the credibility of their arguments. The expertise and authority associated with credible sources can enhance the persuasive impact, as individuals tend to rely on trusted information.

> c) *Consensus and popularity*: Communicators can emphasize the popularity or widespread adoption of

their message or proposed action. People often look to others' behavior as a guide for their own, and highlighting the consensus or popularity of a viewpoint can influence their decisions.

Similarity and Identification:

People tend to be more receptive to messages and ideas presented by individuals they perceive as similar to themselves. Communicators can enhance their persuasive influence by establishing similarity and fostering identification with their audience. Strategies for achieving similarity and identification include:

> a) *Finding common ground*: Effective communicators emphasize shared experiences, beliefs, or goals to create a sense of connection. Identifying commonalities helps bridge the gap between the communicator and the audience, enhancing relatability and increasing the audience's receptiveness to the message.

b) *Using inclusive language*: Communicators can employ language that includes and acknowledges the diversity of their audience. By using inclusive pronouns (e.g., "we," "us") and framing the message in a way that encompasses different perspectives, communicators foster a sense of belonging and identification.

c) *Appealing to self-image*: Persuasive communicators tap into the audience's self-image and aspirations. By aligning the message with the audience's desired identity or self-perception, communicators enhance the persuasive impact. This approach encourages individuals to adopt the communicator's viewpoint or take action to align with their desired self-image.

Scarcity and Urgency:

The scarcity principle suggests that people are motivated by the fear of missing out or the desire to obtain something unique or exclusive. Communicators can leverage scarcity and urgency to increase persuasive influence. Key techniques include:

a) *Limited availability*: By presenting a message or opportunity as having limited availability, communicators create a sense of urgency. This technique taps into the fear of missing out, increasing motivation to act promptly.

b) *Unique benefits or advantages*: Communicators highlight the exclusive benefits or advantages associated with adopting their viewpoint or taking specific action. By emphasizing what sets their proposal apart from alternatives, they create a perception of scarcity and increase the persuasive impact.

c) *Time-sensitive incentives*: Offering time-limited incentives or rewards can enhance persuasion. By creating a sense of urgency through time constraints, communicators motivate individuals to act promptly to obtain the offered benefits

How to persuade within the context of erotism in management

Ethical Considerations in Attraction-Based Persuasion:

While attraction-based persuasion strategies can be highly effective, it is essential to consider ethical principles and responsibilities. Persuasion should never involve manipulation, deception, or exploitation. Communicators must prioritize honesty, transparency, and respect for the autonomy of the audience.

They should provide accurate information, avoid exaggeration, and ensure that individuals have the freedom to make informed choices. The ethical use of attraction-based persuasion strategies fosters trust, builds long-term relationships, and aligns with the principles of ethical communication.

Attraction-based persuasion strategies harness the power of personal connections, emotions, likability, and relatability to influence individuals' opinions and behaviors. By understanding and employing techniques such as establishing rapport, appealing to emotions, leveraging social proof, establishing similarity, and creating a sense of scarcity, communicators can enhance their persuasive influence. However, it is crucial to adhere to ethical principles, ensuring transparency, honesty, and respect for the autonomy of the audience.

By mastering attraction-based persuasion strategies ethically, communicators can achieve greater success in influencing behavior, building relationships, and achieving their desired outcomes.

Creating an Attractive Environment for Collaborators

Creating an attractive environment for collaborators can have a profound impact on their engagement, productivity, and overall satisfaction within the workplace. This concept emphasizes the importance of incorporating elements of attraction, allure, and sensuality to foster a positive and stimulating work environment.

One aspect of creating an attractive environment is paying attention to aesthetics and design. The physical space in which collaborators work can significantly influence their mood, motivation, and creativity.

By carefully considering elements such as colors, lighting, textures, and spatial arrangements, leaders can create an environment that is visually appealing and inspiring. Thoughtful interior design can evoke positive emotions and contribute to a sense of well-being among employees.

Color psychology plays a crucial role in creating an attractive environment. Different colors have the power to evoke specific emotions and moods. For example, warm colors like red, orange, and yellow are known to stimulate energy, creativity, and passion. Cool colors such as blue and green promote calmness, focus, and relaxation. By strategically using colors in the workspace, leaders can create an atmosphere that aligns with the desired outcomes and enhances the overall ambiance.

In addition to colors, lighting is another important aspect of creating an attractive environment. Natural light has been shown to improve mood, productivity, and overall well-being. Incorporating large windows, skylights, or light tubes into the workspace allows for ample natural light to flood the area. If natural light is limited, artificial lighting should be carefully considered. Harsh fluorescent lighting can be detrimental to the atmosphere, while softer and adjustable lighting can create a more comfortable and inviting environment.

The arrangement of furniture and spatial layout also contributes to the overall aesthetics and functionality of the workspace. Open-plan layouts have become increasingly popular as they promote collaboration, communication, and a sense of community among employees. By removing physical barriers and creating shared spaces, colleagues can easily interact and exchange ideas. However, it is also important to provide private or semi-private spaces where individuals can focus on their tasks or hold confidential discussions. A well-balanced combination of open and private spaces can create a dynamic and attractive environment that caters to various work styles and preferences.

Furthermore, incorporating elements of nature and biophilic design can greatly enhance the attractiveness of the workspace. Biophilic design principles involve bringing elements of the natural world into the built environment, such as plants, natural materials, and views of nature. Studies have shown that exposure to nature or natural elements can reduce stress, improve cognitive function, and boost creativity. Introducing greenery, incorporating natural textures and materials, and providing access to outdoor spaces or views can create a more inviting and inspiring atmosphere for collaborators.

Aesthetics alone, however, are not enough to create an attractive environment. Collaborators should have access to workspaces that are engaging and stimulating, supporting their tasks and encouraging collaboration. This can be achieved through the careful design of different work areas that cater to specific needs. Open-plan spaces, for example, promote spontaneous interactions and idea-sharing, while breakout rooms or collaboration zones provide dedicated spaces for team discussions or brainstorming sessions. Quiet areas or designated focus rooms offer solitude and concentration for tasks that require intense focus or privacy.

Comfort is also a crucial aspect of an attractive work environment. Collaborators should have access to ergonomic furniture, adjustable desks, and supportive seating to ensure their physical well-being. Additionally, providing amenities such as cozy lounges, relaxation areas, or even game rooms can contribute to a more enjoyable and attractive work environment. These spaces allow employees to take breaks, recharge, and engage in informal interactions, fostering a sense of camaraderie and well-being.

Moreover, technology and resources play a significant role in creating an attractive environment. Collaborators should be equipped with the necessary tools and technologies that enable them to perform their tasks efficiently and effectively. Outdated or insufficient equipment can hinder productivity and cause frustration. By investing in state-of-the-art technology and providing access to cutting-edge resources, leaders demonstrate their commitment to creating an environment that supports innovation, collaboration, and high-quality work.

Recognition and appreciation are also vital components of creating an attractive environment. Collaborators thrive when they feel valued, recognized, and appreciated for their contributions. Leaders who foster a culture of recognition and appreciation create a positive and motivating atmosphere in the workplace. Regularly acknowledging individual and team achievements helps to cultivate a sense of fulfillment, loyalty, and commitment among employees. This recognition can take various forms, such as public praise during team meetings or company-wide communications, rewards for outstanding performance, or opportunities for professional growth and development. By celebrating successes and milestones, leaders demonstrate to collaborators that their efforts are valued and recognized.

Furthermore, creating opportunities for growth and development is an essential aspect of attracting and engaging collaborators. Employees are more likely to be motivated and satisfied when they feel that their skills and knowledge are being nurtured and expanded.

Leaders should provide access to training programs, workshops, conferences, and mentorship opportunities that enable collaborators to enhance their skills, broaden their horizons, and pursue their professional aspirations.

Supporting career progression and offering clear paths for advancement also contribute to an attractive work environment, as employees feel empowered and motivated to excel in their roles.

Supportive leadership is another crucial aspect of creating an attractive environment for collaborators. Leaders who demonstrate empathy, authenticity, and emotional intelligence contribute to a positive workplace culture. By showing genuine care for their employees' well-being and professional growth, leaders foster a sense of trust, psychological safety, and mutual respect. This supportive leadership encourages open communication, collaboration, and innovation, creating an environment where employees feel empowered to contribute their ideas and talents. Leaders should be approachable, actively listen to their team members' concerns and ideas, and provide guidance and support when needed.

In summary, creating an attractive environment for collaborators involves considering various elements, including aesthetics, engaging workspaces, recognition, resources, and supportive leadership. By integrating elements of attraction, allure, and sensuality into the workplace, leaders can foster a positive and stimulating environment that enhances employee engagement, productivity, and overall satisfaction.

By prioritizing the well-being, growth, and recognition of collaborators, organizations can create an environment that attracts and retains top talent and promotes a positive work culture. Investing in the physical space, incorporating nature, providing comfortable and functional work areas, recognizing achievements, offering opportunities for growth, and demonstrating supportive leadership are all crucial steps in creating an attractive environment that inspires, motivates, and engages collaborators.

Persuasion and Manipulation: Limits and Ethics

Persuasion and manipulation are two concepts often discussed in the context of management and leadership. When considering the use of seduction as a means of persuasion and manipulation in the workplace, it is essential to explore the limits and ethics associated with such practices.

Persuasion can be defined as the act of influencing others' thoughts, beliefs, or actions through logical reasoning, emotional appeal, or the presentation of compelling evidence. It is a legitimate and necessary tool in management, as leaders often need to convince their team members, stakeholders, or clients of certain ideas, strategies, or decisions. Persuasion, when conducted ethically, aims to create mutually beneficial outcomes by presenting valid arguments and respecting the autonomy and free will of individuals.

On the other hand, manipulation involves using tactics or strategies to influence others without their full awareness or informed consent, often for personal gain or to serve one's own agenda. Manipulation is generally considered unethical as it undermines transparency, trust, and the well-being of individuals. It can involve deceit, coercion, or exploiting vulnerabilities to achieve desired outcomes, disregarding the ethical principles of honesty, fairness, and respect for others.

When discussing management by seduction, it is crucial to consider the ethical implications and potential risks associated with this approach. Seduction, in this context, refers to the use of charm, allure, or sensuality to persuade or manipulate others. While the idea of using seduction to achieve business goals may initially appear enticing, it is important to examine the limitations and ethical concerns involved.

Firstly, the use of seduction in management blurs professional boundaries and can lead to inappropriate or exploitative relationships. The workplace should be a space where individuals are treated with respect and dignity, and personal or intimate connections can compromise the fairness, objectivity, and professionalism that should govern professional interactions. Engaging in seductive tactics may create a hostile work environment, undermine trust, and harm the well-being of employees.

Furthermore, relying on seduction as a management strategy can undermine the credibility and integrity of leaders. When persuasion is based solely on superficial charm or physical attractiveness, it neglects the substance and merits of ideas or decisions. This can lead to a culture where manipulation and deception are normalized, eroding trust and fostering an environment of skepticism and disengagement.

Another concern is the potential for seduction to create unequal power dynamics within the workplace. Employees who are subjected to seductive tactics may feel coerced, manipulated, or pressured to comply with requests or decisions that they might otherwise reject. This power imbalance can stifle open communication, discourage dissenting opinions, and impede the free expression of ideas, ultimately hindering innovation and organizational growth.

Moreover, using seduction as a management strategy may perpetuate gender biases and reinforce stereotypes. If seduction is predominantly directed towards a specific gender or if certain individuals are more susceptible to seductive tactics due to cultural or social conditioning, it can perpetuate inequality, discrimination, and a hostile work environment. Organizations should strive to create an inclusive and equitable workplace where individuals are valued for their skills, contributions, and professional merits rather than their physical attributes.

To promote ethical management practices, leaders should focus on building trust, fostering open communication, and creating an environment where diverse perspectives are encouraged and respected. The emphasis should be on clear and transparent communication, logical reasoning, and the presentation of evidence-based arguments. By cultivating a culture of trust, respect, and fairness, leaders can inspire genuine engagement, commitment, and collaboration among their team members.

In conclusion, while persuasion is an essential tool in management, the use of seduction as a means of persuasion and manipulation raises important ethical concerns.

Seductive tactics can undermine professionalism, create unequal power dynamics, perpetuate gender biases, and compromise the well-being of individuals in the workplace. Instead, leaders should prioritize ethical persuasion techniques that respect autonomy, foster trust, and prioritize the merits of ideas and decisions.

By upholding ethical standards, organizations can cultivate a positive work culture that promotes integrity, fairness, and mutual re

Developing Charisma

Developing charisma is a valuable skill that can greatly impact one's effectiveness as a leader and communicator. Charismatic individuals possess a magnetic presence and the ability to inspire and influence others. While some may believe that charisma is an innate quality, it is important to recognize that charisma can be cultivated and developed over time with conscious effort and practice.

One of the key aspects of developing charisma is self-awareness. Understanding oneself, including strengths, weaknesses, values, and beliefs, is crucial in building an authentic and genuine presence. Self-awareness allows individuals to project confidence and clarity, which are attractive qualities in a charismatic leader. Taking the time for self-reflection, seeking feedback from trusted sources, and engaging in personal development activities can enhance self-awareness and contribute to the development of charisma.

Developing self-awareness starts with introspection. It involves exploring one's thoughts, feelings, motivations, and behaviors. Taking time for self-reflection can be achieved through practices such as journaling, meditation, or seeking the guidance of a mentor or coach. By developing a deeper understanding of oneself, individuals can gain insight into their strengths and areas for improvement, leading to a more authentic and charismatic presence.

Seeking feedback from others is another powerful way to enhance self-awareness. Receiving input from trusted colleagues, mentors, or supervisors can provide valuable insights into one's strengths and blind spots. Constructive feedback helps individuals understand how they are perceived by others and identify areas where they can refine their communication, interpersonal skills, or leadership style. Being open to feedback and actively seeking it demonstrates a commitment to personal growth and development, which contributes to the cultivation of charisma.

Engaging in personal development activities is essential for continuous growth and self-improvement. This can include attending workshops or seminars, reading books on leadership and communication, participating in relevant training programs, or seeking opportunities for professional development. These activities allow individuals to broaden their knowledge, learn new skills, and gain fresh perspectives, all of which contribute to the development of charisma.

Another important element of developing charisma is effective communication. Charismatic individuals have the ability to articulate their ideas clearly and persuasively, capturing the attention and interest of others.

They are skilled listeners, paying close attention to the needs and perspectives of those they interact with. Developing strong communication skills involves active listening, empathizing with others, and adapting one's communication style to different audiences. By practicing effective communication, individuals can enhance their charisma and create meaningful connections with others.

Active listening is a foundational skill for effective communication. It involves fully focusing on the speaker, being present in the moment, and suspending judgment. Charismatic individuals actively listen to others, seeking to understand their perspectives, needs, and emotions. They demonstrate empathy by acknowledging and validating the feelings of others, which fosters trust and rapport. Active listening allows individuals to connect on a deeper level, demonstrating respect and creating an environment where others feel heard and valued.

Adapting communication style is also crucial for developing charisma. Different situations and individuals require different approaches to communication. Charismatic individuals are versatile in their communication style, adjusting their tone, language, and delivery to resonate with their audience.

They consider the preferences, cultural backgrounds, and communication styles of others to ensure effective and impactful communication. Adapting communication style demonstrates empathy, flexibility, and the ability to connect with diverse individuals, further enhancing charisma.

Confidence is a characteristic often associated with charisma. Building self-confidence involves recognizing and acknowledging one's strengths, accomplishments, and abilities. It also involves taking risks, stepping outside of one's comfort zone, and embracing challenges. Confidence is contagious, and when individuals exude self-assuredness, they naturally attract and influence others.

Developing confidence requires continuous self-improvement, setting and achieving goals, and celebrating successes along the way.

Building self-confidence starts with acknowledging one's achievements and recognizing personal growth. Taking inventory of past accomplishments, both big and small, helps individuals develop a positive self-image.

By acknowledging and celebrating these successes, individuals reinforce their belief in their abilities and build resilience. It is important to set realistic goals and break them down into manageable steps, celebrating each milestone along the way. This iterative process of setting and achieving goals fosters self-confidence and contributes to the development of charisma.

Stepping outside of one's comfort zone is another powerful way to develop self-confidence. By taking risks and embracing new challenges, individuals expand their comfort zone and discover their true capabilities.

This can involve volunteering for new projects, pursuing leadership roles, or engaging in public speaking opportunities. Stepping outside of one's comfort zone may feel uncomfortable or even intimidating, but it is through these experiences that individuals can grow and develop self-assurance. Learning from setbacks and viewing them as opportunities for growth is essential in building resilience and maintaining confidence.

Authenticity is a vital component of charisma. Charismatic individuals are true to themselves, expressing their values, beliefs, and personality genuinely. They avoid putting on a facade or pretending to be someone they are not. Authenticity creates trust and allows others to connect on a deeper level. To develop authenticity, individuals should focus on embracing their unique qualities, being transparent in their interactions, and aligning their actions with their values. When individuals embrace their true selves, they radiate an aura of authenticity that is compelling to others.

Embracing authenticity starts with a deep understanding of one's values, beliefs, and passions. Identifying core values helps individuals make decisions and take actions that align with their authentic selves.

By living in alignment with their values, individuals demonstrate integrity and create a sense of congruence that is attractive to others. Reflecting on personal experiences, strengths, and passions can help individuals discover their authentic voice and bring their true selves to their interactions and leadership roles.

Transparency is another important aspect of authenticity. Charismatic individuals are open and honest in their communications, sharing their thoughts, feelings, and perspectives genuinely. They avoid hiding information or manipulating others for personal gain. Transparency builds trust and fosters genuine connections. By practicing open and honest communication, individuals create an environment where others feel comfortable doing the same, fostering collaboration, and innovation.

Aligning actions with values is essential for maintaining authenticity. Charismatic individuals walk the talk, ensuring that their behaviors align with their stated values.

This consistency between words and actions creates credibility and trust. It is important to make conscious choices and decisions that reflect one's values, even in challenging situations. This integrity and authenticity inspire others to follow suit and contribute to the development of an authentic and charismatic organizational culture.

Charismatic individuals often possess a positive mindset and a sense of enthusiasm. They are optimistic and inspire others with their energy and passion.

Developing a positive attitude involves cultivating gratitude, focusing on solutions rather than problems, and maintaining resilience in the face of challenges. By fostering a positive mindset, individuals can cultivate charisma and create a motivating and inspiring environment for those around them.

Cultivating gratitude is a powerful practice for developing a positive mindset. Taking time each day to reflect on what one is grateful for can shift the focus from problems to the positive aspects of life. Expressing gratitude to others, whether through words or actions, creates a positive and uplifting environment. By focusing on gratitude, individuals develop a positive outlook and radiate an energy that attracts and inspires others.

Another aspect of developing a positive attitude is focusing on solutions rather than dwelling on problems. Charismatic individuals approach challenges with a proactive mindset, seeking solutions and opportunities for growth.

They view obstacles as learning experiences and steppingstones to success. By reframing problems as opportunities, individuals cultivate resilience and inspire others to adopt a solution-oriented mindset.

Maintaining resilience is crucial for developing a positive attitude. Resilient individuals bounce back from setbacks, adapt to change, and persevere in the face of adversity. Building resilience involves developing coping mechanisms, seeking support from others, and practicing self-care.

By maintaining a resilient mindset, individuals demonstrate determination and inspire others to stay positive and focused on their goals.

Charismatic individuals also possess a keen sense of emotional intelligence. Emotional intelligence refers to the ability to recognize and understand one's own emotions and those of others, and to effectively manage and channel emotions in interactions. Developing emotional intelligence involves practicing empathy, recognizing, and regulating one's own emotions, and navigating social dynamics with sensitivity.

By honing emotional intelligence, individuals can enhance their ability to connect with others on a deeper level, fostering trust and rapport.

Practicing empathy is fundamental to developing emotional intelligence. Empathy involves understanding and sharing the feelings and perspectives of others.

Charismatic individuals listen attentively, seek to understand the emotions of those they interact with, and validate their experiences. By putting themselves in others' shoes, individuals can establish meaningful connections, demonstrate care and understanding, and create a supportive and collaborative environment.

Recognizing and regulating one's own emotions is another key aspect of emotional intelligence. Charismatic individuals have self-awareness when it comes to their emotional states and can manage their emotions effectively. This involves recognizing triggers, managing stress, and responding to situations with emotional intelligence. By remaining calm and composed in challenging situations, individuals inspire confidence and earn the respect of others.

Navigating social dynamics with sensitivity is essential for developing emotional intelligence.

Charismatic individuals are attuned to the social cues and dynamics within a group. They adapt their behavior and communication style to connect with diverse individuals and create inclusive environments. By demonstrating sensitivity and respect for cultural differences, diverse perspectives, and individual preferences, individuals enhance their emotional intelligence and create connections that transcend differences.

In conclusion, developing charisma is a multifaceted process that involves self-awareness, effective communication, confidence, authenticity, positivity, and emotional intelligence.

By focusing on these aspects and continuously investing in personal growth and development, individuals can cultivate their own unique brand of charisma, positively influencing and inspiring others in their personal and professional lives.

Developing charisma requires self-reflection, seeking feedback, engaging in personal development activities, active listening, adapting communication style, building confidence, embracing authenticity, fostering a positive mindset, and honing emotional intelligence. With dedication and practice, individuals can develop and enhance their charisma, contributing to their success as leaders and communicators.

Identifying and Enhancing Charismatic Traits

Identifying and enhancing charismatic traits is an important endeavor for individuals seeking to develop their leadership skills and influence others effectively. Charisma is often seen as a quality that some individuals naturally possess, but it is also a set of characteristics that can be nurtured and cultivated over time.

One of the key aspects of identifying charismatic traits is self-reflection. Taking the time to introspect and understand one's own strengths and weaknesses is essential in recognizing areas for development. This involves reflecting on one's communication style, emotional intelligence, confidence, and presence.

Self-reflection can be facilitated through practices such as journaling, meditation, or seeking the guidance of a mentor or coach. By examining one's thoughts, actions, and impact on others, individuals can gain valuable insights into their charismatic potential.

Effective communication is a fundamental charismatic trait. Charismatic individuals possess the ability to articulate their ideas clearly, passionately, and persuasively. They have a compelling presence that captivates and engages their audience.

Developing effective communication skills involves not only the clarity and fluency of speech but also the ability to listen actively and empathetically. Charismatic individuals are skilled listeners who genuinely connect with others, show empathy, and respond thoughtfully. By improving communication skills through practice, individuals can enhance their charisma and inspire others.

Confidence is another characteristic often associated with charisma. Charismatic individuals exude self-assurance and project a strong sense of belief in themselves and their ideas. Building confidence starts with recognizing one's strengths, accomplishments, and capabilities.

It involves acknowledging past successes and using them as a foundation to tackle new challenges. Stepping outside of one's comfort zone and embracing opportunities for growth can also boost confidence. By taking risks and pushing boundaries, individuals expand their capabilities and cultivate the confidence needed to be charismatic leaders.

Charismatic individuals possess authenticity, which is the ability to be genuine and true to oneself. Authenticity creates trust and credibility, allowing others to connect on a deeper level. Being authentic requires self-awareness and self-acceptance. It involves embracing one's values, beliefs, and unique qualities. Charismatic individuals avoid putting on a facade or pretending to be someone they are not.

By staying true to their authentic selves, individuals demonstrate integrity and create an environment where others feel safe to express themselves.

Emotional intelligence is a crucial charismatic trait. It involves understanding and managing one's own emotions and being attuned to the emotions of others. Charismatic individuals have the ability to empathize with others, recognizing their needs, perspectives, and feelings.

This empathy allows them to connect with others on an emotional level and build meaningful relationships. Developing emotional intelligence requires self-awareness, self-regulation, social awareness, and relationship management. By honing these skills, individuals can enhance their charisma and effectively influence others.

Charismatic individuals often possess a positive mindset and a sense of enthusiasm. They radiate optimism, energy, and passion, inspiring those around them.

Developing a positive attitude involves cultivating gratitude, focusing on solutions rather than dwelling on problems, and maintaining resilience in the face of challenges. By embracing positivity and demonstrating resilience, individuals can attract and motivate others, contributing to their overall charisma.

Continual growth and learning are vital for enhancing charismatic traits. This involves seeking feedback from trusted sources, attending workshops or seminars, reading books on leadership and communication, and engaging in self-development activities. By actively pursuing opportunities for personal and professional growth, individuals can refine their charismatic skills and further develop their potential.

Another aspect of developing charisma is cultivating a strong presence. Charismatic individuals have a commanding presence that draws others in and captures their attention. They exude confidence, poise, and authenticity.

Developing a strong presence involves practicing good body language, maintaining eye contact, and projecting a calm and assertive demeanor. It also requires being fully present in interactions and actively engaging with others. By honing their presence, individuals can enhance their charisma and make a lasting impression on those they interact with.

Building strong relationships and fostering connections is another key element of developing charisma. Charismatic individuals excel in building rapport and establishing trust with others.

They take a genuine interest in people, actively listen to their concerns, and demonstrate empathy. By focusing on building meaningful connections, individuals can cultivate charisma and create a supportive and collaborative environment.

Additionally, charisma is closely tied to effective leadership. Charismatic leaders inspire and motivate their team members, creating a shared sense of purpose and vision. They possess the ability to communicate a compelling vision, instill confidence, and mobilize others towards achieving common goals. Charismatic leaders also empower their team members, fostering a sense of autonomy and ownership. By developing leadership skills, individuals can amplify their charisma and have a greater impact on those around them.

While developing charismatic traits is essential, it is important to maintain authenticity and ethical practices. Charisma should be used responsibly and with genuine intentions.

Manipulating or exploiting others for personal gain goes against the principles of charisma.

Instead, charismatic individuals should focus on creating positive and inclusive environments, inspiring others, and fostering growth and development.

In conclusion, identifying and enhancing charismatic traits is a valuable pursuit for individuals aspiring to become influential leaders.

By engaging in self-reflection, developing effective communication skills, building confidence, embracing authenticity, cultivating emotional intelligence, maintaining a positive mindset, and pursuing continuous growth, individuals can strengthen their charisma and positively impact those around them.

Charismatic traits can be nurtured and developed through practice, self-awareness, and a genuine desire to connect with and inspire others. By embodying charisma, individuals can become effective leaders and make a lasting impression in their personal and professional lives.

Empathy and Emotional Connection in Management

Empathy and emotional connection play integral roles in effective management. They are essential in building strong relationships, fostering collaboration, and creating a positive work environment.

In this extensive discussion, we will explore the significance of empathy and emotional connection in management and how they contribute to individual and organizational success.

Empathy, often described as the ability to understand and share the feelings of others, is a fundamental skill for managers. It involves actively listening to employees, demonstrating understanding, and considering their perspectives.

By putting themselves in others' shoes, empathetic managers can gain valuable insights into the needs, concerns, and motivations of their team members. This understanding allows them to respond with compassion, provide support, and create a sense of psychological safety in the workplace.

Empathy in management begins with active listening. It involves giving full attention to what others are saying, without interrupting or passing judgment. Through active listening, managers can comprehend the emotions behind the words, uncover underlying issues, and demonstrate their commitment to understanding and supporting their employees.

When team members feel heard and understood, they are more likely to feel valued and motivated to contribute to the organization's success.

Another aspect of empathy is demonstrating understanding and validation. Empathetic managers acknowledge the emotions expressed by their employees and show empathy by validating their experiences.

This can be achieved through verbal affirmation, such as saying, "I understand how you feel" or "I appreciate your perspective." It is important for managers to create a safe space where individuals feel comfortable expressing their emotions and concerns without fear of judgment or reprisal.

By validating their emotions, managers foster trust, encourage open communication, and strengthen emotional connections.

Empathy goes beyond understanding and validation; it also involves taking action. Empathetic managers proactively support their employees by providing resources, guidance, and encouragement.

They strive to address any challenges or obstacles faced by their team members and actively seek solutions. By demonstrating empathy through action, managers create a culture of care and support, enhancing employee morale, engagement, and well-being.

In addition to empathy, emotional connection is crucial in management. Emotional connection refers to the ability to forge deep and meaningful relationships with employees based on trust, respect, and shared values.

It involves creating an environment where individuals feel comfortable expressing their emotions, sharing their ideas, and being their authentic selves. Emotional connection is the foundation for effective collaboration, open communication, and high-performing teams.

Building emotional connections starts with authenticity. Managers who are authentic in their interactions create an environment where employees feel safe to be themselves. Authenticity involves expressing genuine emotions, sharing personal experiences when appropriate, and being transparent about intentions and decisions.

When employees perceive their managers as authentic, they are more likely to reciprocate with trust and authenticity, fostering strong emotional connections.

Trust is a fundamental component of emotional connection. Managers must cultivate trust by consistently demonstrating integrity, reliability, and accountability. Trust is built through open communication, keeping promises, and providing constructive feedback. When employees trust their managers, they feel comfortable sharing their ideas, concerns, and challenges. This openness facilitates collaboration and innovation, leading to improved problem-solving and decision-making.

Respect is another key element in developing emotional connections. Managers must treat employees with respect, valuing their contributions, perspectives, and diverse backgrounds.

Respecting employees' individuality fosters a sense of belonging, inclusion, and psychological safety. When employees feel respected, they are more likely to engage fully in their work, share their opinions, and take ownership of their responsibilities.

Emotional connection also requires managers to be emotionally intelligent. Emotional intelligence involves recognizing and understanding one's own emotions and those of others.

Emotionally intelligent managers are attuned to the emotional needs of their employees and respond appropriately. They are self-aware, able to regulate their emotions in challenging situations, and empathetic towards the emotions expressed by others.

By demonstrating emotional intelligence, managers can establish deeper connections, enhance collaboration, and promote a positive work environment. They are mindful of their own emotions, ensuring that they do not allow personal biases or frustrations to hinder effective communication and decision-making.

Emotionally intelligent managers also take into account the emotions of their team members, adapting their approach and providing support when needed.

Developing empathy and emotional connections in management requires ongoing effort and self-reflection.

Managers can enhance their empathy skills by practicing active listening, seeking feedback, and engaging in empathy-building exercises. They can also develop emotional connections by investing time in building relationships, fostering open communication, and promoting a supportive and inclusive work culture.

The benefits of cultivating empathy and emotional connection in management are numerous. Employees who feel understood, valued, and emotionally connected to their managers are more likely to be engaged, motivated, and committed to their work.

They experience greater job satisfaction, which leads to increased productivity and retention rates. Furthermore, empathetic and emotionally connected managers create an environment that encourages creativity, collaboration, and innovation. They foster a sense of shared purpose, leading to high-performing teams and organizational success.

In conclusion, empathy and emotional connection are vital components of effective management. By practicing empathy, managers can understand and address the needs of their employees, fostering trust and psychological safety.

Emotional connection builds strong relationships, promotes collaboration, and creates a positive work environment.

Developing empathy and emotional connection requires active listening, validation, action, authenticity, trust, respect, and emotional intelligence. When managers prioritize these qualities, they cultivate engaged employees, high-performing teams, and organizational success.

Personal Magnetism and Its Influence on the Team

Personal magnetism is a quality that individuals possess that draws others towards them. It is an intangible yet powerful force that influences and captivates those around them.

In the context of a team, personal magnetism can have a significant impact on team dynamics, collaboration, and overall success. In this extensive discussion, we will explore the concept of personal magnetism and its influence on the team.

Personal magnetism encompasses a range of qualities that make an individual compelling and influential. It involves a combination of charisma, presence, authenticity, confidence, and the ability to connect with others on a deep level. Individuals with personal magnetism have a certain "it" factor that attracts and engages others, creating a magnetic pull that draws people towards them.

One of the key components of personal magnetism is charisma. Charismatic individuals possess a unique charm and magnetism that captivates those around them. They have a natural ability to inspire, influence, and motivate others. Charismatic individuals possess excellent communication skills, which allow them to articulate their ideas persuasively and with passion.

They have a commanding presence that commands attention and leaves a lasting impression on others. Charisma helps foster trust and rapport, making it easier to build strong connections within a team.

Authenticity is another essential aspect of personal magnetism. Authentic individuals are true to themselves, expressing their values, beliefs, and personality genuinely. They avoid putting on a façade or pretending to be someone they are not. Authenticity creates trust and allows others to connect on a deeper level. Team members are more likely to be receptive and open to a leader who is authentic, as it establishes a sense of credibility and reliability.

Confidence is a characteristic closely associated with personal magnetism. Confident individuals exude self-assurance and project a strong belief in themselves and their abilities. This confidence inspires trust and instills confidence in others. Confident leaders create a positive and motivating atmosphere within the team, encouraging team members to take risks, share their ideas, and contribute to the team's success.

Presence is another attribute that contributes to personal magnetism. Individuals with a strong presence have a commanding aura that captures attention and influences others. They possess a natural ability to engage and connect with people, making them influential within a team setting. Presence involves being fully present in the moment, actively listening, and showing genuine interest in others. A leader with a strong presence can inspire and energize the team, creating a dynamic and collaborative environment.

Building personal magnetism also requires the ability to connect with others on an emotional level. This emotional connection is fostered through empathy and understanding. Leaders with personal magnetism are attuned to the emotions and needs of their team members, demonstrating empathy and compassion. They actively listen, validate feelings, and respond thoughtfully. By building emotional connections, leaders create a sense of belonging and psychological safety within the team, encouraging open communication and collaboration.

Another aspect of personal magnetism is the ability to inspire and motivate others. Leaders with personal magnetism have a vision and a passion that they convey to the team. They are adept at inspiring others, creating a shared sense of purpose, and mobilizing the team towards a common goal.

Their enthusiasm and passion are contagious, motivating team members to perform at their best and go the extra mile. Through their ability to inspire, leaders with personal magnetism cultivate a high-performing team and drive success.

Personal magnetism can also influence team dynamics in terms of communication and collaboration. Individuals with personal magnetism have a natural ability to foster open and transparent communication within the team.

They create an environment where team members feel comfortable sharing their ideas, opinions, and concerns. This open communication promotes collaboration and the free exchange of ideas, leading to enhanced creativity and problem-solving.

Additionally, personal magnetism can contribute to the development of a positive team culture. Leaders with personal magnetism create a supportive and inclusive environment where team members feel valued, respected, and empowered. They promote a culture of trust, collaboration, and growth, encouraging individuals to reach their full potential. This positive team culture boosts morale, engagement, and overall team performance.

Leaders with personal magnetism are often seen as role models within the team. Their ability to inspire and engage others encourages team members to strive for excellence and personal growth. They create a sense of unity and purpose, fostering a strong team spirit. Team members feel motivated and empowered to contribute their best efforts, knowing that their leader values their input and supports their development.

In addition to its impact on team dynamics, personal magnetism also plays a significant role in attracting and retaining top talent. Individuals are naturally drawn to leaders with personal magnetism. They are inspired by their vision, captivated by their charisma, and motivated by their passion.

This magnetic pull makes the team an attractive and desirable environment to work in. As a result, teams led by individuals with personal magnetism tend to attract high-performing individuals who are eager to contribute and grow within the team.

Moreover, personal magnetism can have a positive effect on conflict resolution within the team. Leaders with personal magnetism have the ability to navigate difficult situations with tact, empathy, and diplomacy. Their presence and influence help diffuse tension and foster a collaborative approach to resolving conflicts.

By encouraging open communication and considering the perspectives of all team members, leaders with personal magnetism create an environment where conflicts can be addressed constructively, leading to improved team dynamics and stronger relationships.

The development of personal magnetism is a lifelong journey that requires self-awareness, continuous learning, and practice. Leaders can enhance their personal magnetism by cultivating their communication skills, developing their emotional intelligence, building self-confidence, and seeking feedback from others.

Engaging in personal growth activities such as self-reflection, coaching, and training programs can also contribute to the development of personal magnetism.

In summary, personal magnetism is a powerful quality that influences and captivates others. Individuals with personal magnetism possess charisma, authenticity, confidence, presence, and the ability to connect with others on a deep level. In a team setting, personal magnetism can have a profound impact on team dynamics, collaboration, and overall success. Leaders with personal magnetism inspire, motivate, and create a positive team culture.

They foster open communication, encourage collaboration, and drive the team towards shared goals. Developing personal magnetism requires self-awareness, authenticity, confidence-building, emotional intelligence, and the ability to inspire and connect with others. By cultivating personal magnetism, leaders can create a magnetic pull that draws their team together and propels them towards success.

Leadership and Sensuality

Leadership and sensuality may seem like unrelated concepts at first glance, but when explored deeply, they reveal powerful connections that can enhance the effectiveness and impact of leaders. Sensuality refers to engaging and stimulating the senses, creating an environment that is rich in sensory experiences.

When leaders incorporate elements of sensuality into their leadership approach, they can cultivate deeper connections, inspire creativity, and foster a positive and engaging work culture.

In this extensive discussion, we will delve into the relationship between leadership and sensuality, and how it can contribute to the success of individuals and organizations.

One aspect of leadership that can be influenced by sensuality is communication. Sensual leaders understand the power of effective communication and recognize that it extends beyond mere words. They utilize a variety of senses to convey their message, creating a more impactful and memorable experience for their team members. This can involve the use of body language, tone of voice, and facial expressions to express emotions and intentions. By engaging the senses in communication, leaders can create a deeper connection with their team, leading to improved understanding and engagement.

Furthermore, sensuality in leadership can be expressed through the physical environment. Sensual leaders pay attention to the aesthetics and ambiance of the workspace, creating an environment that is visually appealing and evokes positive emotions.

This can include incorporating elements such as warm lighting, comfortable seating, and visually pleasing artwork. By designing a space that stimulates the senses, leaders create an atmosphere that encourages creativity, collaboration, and overall well-being.

In addition to the physical environment, sensuality in leadership extends to the use of sensory experiences in team activities and rituals. Leaders can incorporate activities that engage different senses, such as team-building exercises that involve touch or taste, or engaging in mindfulness practices that focus on sensory awareness.

By involving the senses in team activities, leaders create a more immersive and engaging experience, fostering a sense of connection and unity among team members.

Sensual leaders also recognize the importance of emotional intelligence in their interactions with others. Emotional intelligence involves the ability to understand and manage one's own emotions, as well as the emotions of others.

Sensual leaders cultivate emotional intelligence by being attuned to the emotional needs of their team members, showing empathy, and creating a safe space for open expression of emotions.

They understand that emotions play a significant role in human connections and that acknowledging and embracing emotions can strengthen relationships and trust within the team.

Moreover, sensuality in leadership can be expressed through the appreciation and celebration of individual and team achievements. Sensual leaders understand the importance of recognition and acknowledgment in fostering motivation and engagement.

They create rituals or ceremonies that engage the senses to celebrate successes, such as creating visually appealing award presentations or incorporating music and dance into recognition events. By engaging the senses in celebrations, leaders create a memorable and uplifting experience that reinforces a positive and supportive work culture.

Sensual leaders also recognize the power of sensory experiences in driving innovation and creativity within their teams. They understand that sensory stimulation can inspire new ideas and perspectives.

Sensual leaders may encourage their team members to explore different environments, engage in sensory-rich activities, or even incorporate elements of playfulness and experimentation in the workplace. By embracing the sensual aspects of creativity, leaders create an environment that nurtures innovation and encourages team members to think outside the box.

Furthermore, sensuality in leadership involves being present and fully engaged in the present moment. Sensual leaders understand that true connection and meaningful interactions happen when they are fully present with their team members.

They actively listen, show genuine interest, and engage in conversations with undivided attention. By being fully present, leaders create an atmosphere of trust, respect, and authenticity, which allows for deeper connections and effective collaboration.

Sensual leadership also encompasses the ability to tap into the senses to inspire and motivate others. Leaders who embrace sensuality understand that motivation is not solely driven by rationality and logic but also by emotions and sensory experiences. They utilize storytelling techniques that engage the senses to convey their vision and values, and they leverage sensory cues to create memorable experiences that inspire and drive action. By appealing to the senses, leaders can create a lasting impact and instill a sense of purpose and motivation within their team.

Moreover, sensuality in leadership involves the ability to cultivate a positive and inclusive work culture. Sensual leaders prioritize creating an environment where team members feel valued, respected, and empowered. They recognize the importance of sensory experiences in fostering a sense of belonging and engagement.

This can involve incorporating elements such as team meals, social gatherings, or even incorporating sensory elements in team retreats or off-site meetings. By engaging the senses and creating opportunities for team members to connect and bond, leaders cultivate a positive and supportive work culture.

Leadership and sensuality are interconnected in various ways. Sensuality in leadership involves engaging the senses to create deeper connections, inspire creativity, and foster a positive work culture. By incorporating elements of sensuality in communication, the physical environment, team activities, emotional intelligence, recognition and celebration, fostering innovation, being fully present, and motivating others, leaders can enhance their effectiveness and create a more engaging and fulfilling work experience for their team members.

Sensual leadership recognizes the power of sensory experiences in creating meaningful connections, driving motivation, and inspiring innovation, ultimately contributing to the success and well-being of individuals and organizations.

Inspiring Through Desire

Inspiration is a powerful force that drives individuals to go beyond their limits, pursue their passions, and achieve remarkable feats. It is the spark that ignites the fire within, propelling individuals to take action and pursue their goals with unwavering determination. While there are various ways to inspire others, one particularly potent approach is to inspire through desire.

By tapping into the deepest desires and aspirations of individuals, leaders can evoke a sense of purpose, motivation, and unwavering commitment.

In this section, we will explore the concept of inspiring through desire, its psychological underpinnings, and its transformative impact on individuals and organizations.

At the core of inspiring through desire lies the understanding that human motivation is driven by a complex interplay of needs, wants, and aspirations. People are motivated by their desires for growth, fulfillment, and self-actualization.

Leaders who recognize this fundamental truth can tap into the inherent desires of individuals, aligning their goals and aspirations with the larger purpose of the organization. By inspiring through desire, leaders create a powerful emotional connection that transcends mere monetary incentives and taps into the deeper yearnings of individuals.

To inspire through desire, leaders must first understand the individual motivations of their team members. Each person is driven by unique desires and aspirations, and effective leaders take the time to listen, observe, and engage in meaningful conversations to uncover these underlying desires.

By showing genuine interest in their team members' personal goals and aspirations, leaders create a sense of trust and respect.

This lays the foundation for an inspiring leadership approach that aligns individual desires with the collective goals of the organization.

One key psychological principle that underlies inspiring through desire is the concept of self-determination theory. According to this theory, individuals have three basic psychological needs: autonomy, competence, and relatedness.

Autonomy refers to the need to feel in control of one's actions and decisions. Competence relates to the desire to feel capable and effective in one's pursuits. Relatedness involves the need for meaningful connections and a sense of belonging.

Leaders who understand and nurture these basic psychological needs can inspire through desire by creating an environment that supports autonomy, encourages growth and development, and fosters a sense of belonging.

Inspiring through desire also requires leaders to effectively communicate and articulate a compelling vision. A visionary leader can paint a vivid picture of the future, inspiring others to join them on the journey towards that desired outcome.

By clearly articulating the purpose, values, and aspirations of the organization, leaders tap into the desires of individuals to contribute to something meaningful and impactful. This shared sense of purpose and alignment of desires fuels motivation, dedication, and a collective drive towards success.

In addition to effective communication, leaders who inspire through desire embody the qualities of passion, authenticity, and vulnerability. Passion is contagious and has the power to ignite the passions of others. When leaders demonstrate unwavering enthusiasm and dedication to their own desires and goals, they inspire others to do the same.

Authenticity is equally important, as it fosters trust and creates a genuine connection. Leaders who openly share their own desires, challenges, and vulnerabilities create a safe space for others to do the same, encouraging authenticity and deeper connections within the team.

Furthermore, inspiring through desire involves creating a supportive and empowering environment. Leaders must provide the necessary resources, guidance, and opportunities for growth that allow individuals to pursue their desires.

This may involve providing training and development programs, mentoring opportunities, or creating a culture that encourages experimentation and risk-taking. When individuals feel supported in their pursuit of their desires, they are more likely to be motivated, engaged, and committed to achieving their goals.

Inspiring through desire is not limited to individual aspirations but extends to collective aspirations as well. Effective leaders inspire teams to work towards shared desires and goals, fostering a sense of camaraderie, collaboration, and mutual support.

By creating a shared vision and fostering an environment of inclusivity, leaders can align the desires of individuals within the team towards a common purpose. This collective pursuit of shared desires can lead to remarkable outcomes, as the combined efforts and energies of individuals synergize towards a greater goal.

Moreover, inspiring through desire requires leaders to create a culture that celebrates and recognizes the achievements and progress made by individuals and teams. Acknowledging and celebrating successes not only motivates individuals but also reinforces the alignment between their desires and the organizational goals.

Recognition can take various forms, such as public praise, rewards, opportunities for growth, or simply creating a culture of appreciation and gratitude. When individuals feel valued and recognized for their efforts, they are inspired to continue their pursuit of their desires and contribute to the success of the organization.

The concept of inspiring through desire is a powerful tool in organizational development and growth. It's a concept that bridges the gap between personal motivations and professional goals, paving the way for a harmonious, dynamic, and productive work environment.

When desire is effectively channeled, it doesn't merely exist as a personal, detached emotion; rather, it becomes a collective force propelling the organization towards innovation and excellence.

When we talk about organizations embracing the approach of inspiring through desire, it goes beyond the simple act of motivating employees. It is about igniting a spark that fuels their creativity, their willingness to take risks, and their ability to challenge the status quo.

Desire, in this context, is more than a fleeting whim or temporary ambition. It is a deep-seated urge that drives individuals to explore the bounds of their creativity and push the limits of their potential.

One of the many benefits of this approach is the heightened level of innovation within the organization. When individuals are inspired by their desires, they are not restricted by conventional thought patterns or traditional methods of operation.

Instead, they become more open to exploring new ideas, testing uncharted waters, and taking calculated risks. This openness to innovation can lead to breakthrough ideas, improved processes, and unique problem-solving strategies, giving the organization a competitive edge in the market.

However, the impact of this approach is not limited to innovation. Organizations that inspire through desire also tend to witness a surge in productivity. When individuals are driven by their desires, they are naturally more engaged in their work.

This heightened engagement often translates into increased productivity, as individuals are more focused, more motivated, and more committed to their tasks. They aren't merely working to meet targets or deadlines, but they are working towards fulfilling their own desires, which adds an additional layer of motivation and dedication to their work.

Creating a culture where desire is recognized, appreciated, and harnessed can have significant effects on the overall work environment. In such an environment, individuals feel valued, engaged, and connected. They understand that their desires align with the organization's goals and this alignment fosters a sense of belonging and commitment.

Moreover, such a positive work culture significantly contributes to higher levels of job satisfaction. When employees are satisfied, they are less likely to leave the organization, leading to lower turnover rates and higher employee retention.

Inspiring through desire is a transformative leadership approach that taps into the intrinsic motivations of individuals. By understanding and aligning with the desires and aspirations of their team members, leaders can create a powerful emotional connection and foster a sense of purpose, motivation, and unwavering commitment.

Through effective communication, visionary leadership, passion, authenticity, and creating a supportive environment, leaders inspire individuals and teams to pursue their desires and achieve remarkable outcomes.

The impact of inspiring through desire extends beyond individual motivation to organizational success, fostering innovation, productivity, and a positive work culture. By embracing this approach, leaders can unlock the full potential of their team members and create a thriving and fulfilling work environment.

Creating a Stimulating and Motivating Work Environment

The interplay of trust, desire, emotional connection, communication, recognition, and growth - all of which are inherent in the concept of erotism - create a potent cocktail that can fundamentally change how a workplace functions and feels.

When harnessed, this power transforms teams into more than just collections of individuals working together. It metamorphosizes them into dynamic, emotionally connected units working towards a shared vision with purpose, passion, and vigor.

Let us delve deeper into the elements that make up this cocktail. It starts with building trust, which serves as the foundation of all relationships, professional or personal. In a work environment, trust can be built by leaders showing vulnerability, demonstrating that they are not infallible and that they, too, are part of the learning and growing process.

Leaders must also show that they trust their employees, allowing them the freedom to take calculated risks, make decisions, and own their successes and failures. Such actions communicate to the team that the leader believes in their abilities, further strengthening the bonds of trust.

However, the concept of desire goes beyond this. Desire is a powerful human motivator, driving individuals to action. It is not about physical attraction, but the aspiration to be part of something meaningful, to contribute, to grow. Leaders can channel this desire towards achieving a shared vision by creating and communicating a compelling, shared vision that aligns with their team's values and aspirations.

Creating such a vision demands that leaders understand their teams at a deeper, more personal level. This involves understanding their dreams, their values, their motivations, their fears, and their challenges. It requires leaders to show empathy, not as a tactic but as a genuine human emotion.

This empathy fosters a strong emotional connection, an erotic bond, between the leader and the team, driving the team to commit to their shared vision with unwavering dedication and motivation.

Communication is the medium through which this vision is shared and the emotional connection is fostered. Effective communication involves articulating thoughts and ideas clearly, and, more importantly, actively listening and responding with understanding. By practicing empathetic communication, leaders can cultivate an environment where everyone feels heard, understood, and valued. This type of communication resonates at an emotional level, striking a chord with employees and enhancing their motivation and engagement.

Erotic communication goes beyond words. It involves a deeper, more intimate level of engagement. It is about being present, being in the moment, and genuinely connecting with the other person. When leaders communicate in this way, it sends a strong message to employees that they matter, that their work matters, which significantly enhances their motivation to perform.

The role of recognition in creating a motivating work environment cannot be understated. Recognition is not merely about praising achievements; it is about appreciating the effort, the progress, and the individual's unique contribution to the team.

When leaders recognize their employees authentically and consistently, they create a positive feedback loop that reinforces positive behavior and encourages continuous effort and improvement. This form of recognition fulfills a deep human need to feel appreciated and valued, creating an environment that is motivating and high performing.

However, recognition must be coupled with opportunities for learning and growth to truly create a stimulating work environment. This means providing challenging assignments that stretch the employees, providing constructive feedback that helps them learn and grow, and offering opportunities for professional development. By fulfilling this basic human need for growth, leaders can significantly enhance their team's motivation and job satisfaction.

Moreover, leaders can cultivate a sense of sensuality in the work environment by creating an atmosphere that stimulates the senses. This could be through aesthetic elements like a well-designed workspace, or through activities that encourage employees to engage with their senses.

This approach can foster a deeper, more intimate connection with the work environment, making work a more enjoyable and motivating experience.

The concept of erotism in business management may seem unconventional and even controversial to some. But when understood and applied correctly, it can unleash a powerful force that drives teams towards exceptional performance and success. It provides a new lens through which we can view and approach management - a lens that sees beyond the tasks and processes to the human element that drives it all.

The transformative power of erotism lies in its ability to stimulate and motivate through deep human connection, desire, trust, communication, recognition, and growth. By harnessing this power, leaders can create work environments that are not only highly productive but also deeply satisfying and fulfilling.

In essence, creating a stimulating and motivating work environment using erotism in business management is about understanding, appreciating, and harnessing the power of human nature. It's about seeing employees as whole human beings with desires, emotions, and aspirations.

It's about building meaningful, emotionally engaging relationships. It's about creating an environment where people feel valued, where they are motivated to give their best, and where they find joy and fulfillment in their work. This is the art and science of *Seducing Success* in the world of business.

Erotic Leadership as a Strategy for Success

Delving deeper into the text, the concept of 'Erotic Leadership as a Strategy for Success' demonstrates a profound shift from traditional, transactional leadership styles toward a more holistic approach that embraces the multi-dimensional nature of human beings.

The text begins by setting the stage in the realm of leadership, contrasting the objective, rational nature of the business world with the emotional, aspirational, and connection-oriented nature of human beings.

This contrast is integral to the philosophy of erotic leadership, which posits that leaders can achieve greater success by acknowledging and harnessing the emotional, passionate side of human nature.

The first key concept discussed is desire. Desire, as presented here, is not limited to physical or romantic aspirations but extends to a broader spectrum of human motivation, including the desire for achievement, growth, connection, and recognition. Desire propels human action and thus can be a potent driving force within the context of leadership. Leaders who understand the desires of their team members can align these aspirations with the organization's goals, creating a shared vision that the entire team is motivated to pursue.

The concept of a shared vision is central to erotic leadership. Rather than being a set of objectives or a strategic plan, a shared vision is an emotionally engaging idea that resonates with the team members' aspirations and values. Crafting such a vision requires a deep understanding of the team and effective communication to connect with team members emotionally.

The next key concept the text explores is erotic communication. This concept goes beyond the mere transmission of information. Instead, it emphasizes creating emotional connections through communication. It includes being present, authentic, and empathetic. Erotic leaders understand the power of their words, tone, body language, and actions in influencing and inspiring their team members.

Active listening, a component of erotic communication, is presented as a powerful tool for building connections. It demonstrates to team members that their thoughts and opinions are valued and contributes to enhancing their sense of belonging and commitment to the team.

The text then moves on to the concepts of trust and respect. Trust is portrayed as a fundamental cornerstone of any relationship, and in the context of leadership, it is built by being reliable, consistent, transparent, and fair. By trusting their team members and showing that they trust them, erotic leaders foster an environment where people feel comfortable expressing their thoughts and taking risks.

Respect, another facet of erotic leadership, involves valuing each person as an individual with unique strengths, perspectives, and experiences. Erotic leaders encourage diversity and inclusivity, understanding that they can lead to better decision-making and more innovative solutions.

Recognition and appreciation are also powerful tools in the erotic leader's toolkit. Recognizing people's efforts and achievements makes them feel valued and appreciated, enhancing their self-esteem, motivation, and commitment to the team.

The creation of a stimulating work environment is another strategy employed by erotic leaders. They understand that motivation goes beyond financial rewards. By creating an enjoyable, challenging, and meaningful work environment that offers opportunities for learning and growth, erotic leaders inspire their team members to contribute their best.

The text also emphasizes the importance of emotional well-being. Erotic leaders foster a culture where emotional intelligence is valued, and people feel comfortable expressing their emotions. By being aware of their own emotions and showing empathy toward their team's feelings, erotic leaders contribute to a positive, supportive work environment where people feel understood and valued.

Finally, the text highlights the significance of leading by example in erotic leadership. Erotic leaders embody the values, behaviors, and attitudes they want their team members to emulate. They show that they are part of the team working towards a shared vision, inspiring their team members, and earning their respect and admiration.

In summary, erotic leadership is a transformative approach to leadership that acknowledges and harnesses the emotional, passionate side of human nature. It is a strategy that holds immense potential for enhancing the motivation, commitment, and performance of teams, and ultimately driving business success.

Looking at these concepts in isolation, each provides a new dimension of understanding to the realm of leadership. However, when considered together, they form a cohesive, powerful framework for leadership that can bring about profound shifts in how leaders engage with their teams and drive success in their organizations.

At its core, erotic leadership is about embracing the human side of business. It acknowledges that businesses, despite their focus on objectivity and rationality, are, in reality, driven by human beings with their own sets of desires, emotions, and need for connection. By recognizing this fact and harnessing these aspects of human nature, erotic leaders can create a more engaged, motivated, and high-performing team.

Understanding desire and creating a shared vision based on this understanding are central to the concept of erotic leadership.

By aligning the individual desires of team members with the overarching goals of the organization, leaders can craft a shared vision that resonates with the team on an emotional level, fostering a high level of commitment and motivation to work towards this vision.

Erotic communication and active listening play key roles in this process. By being present, authentic, and empathetic, and by truly listening to understand, erotic leaders can create powerful emotional connections with their teams.

These connections enhance team members' sense of belonging and commitment to the team and the shared vision.

Trust and respect are fundamental to the concept of erotic leadership. By building trust and demonstrating respect for each team member, erotic leaders create an inclusive environment where people feel safe to express their thoughts, take risks, and bring their full selves to work.

Recognition and appreciation are also integral to the erotic leadership approach. By recognizing and appreciating the efforts and achievements of team members, erotic leaders can enhance team members' self-esteem, motivation, and commitment to the team and the shared vision.

The creation of a stimulating work environment and the focus on emotional well-being further contribute to the effectiveness of the erotic leadership approach. By creating an enjoyable, challenging, and meaningful work environment, and by verifying and fostering emotional expression and well-being, erotic leaders can inspire their teams to bring their best selves to work.

Leading by example is a powerful tool in the erotic leadership toolkit. By embodying the desired values, behaviors, and attitudes, erotic leaders inspire their teams and earn their respect and admiration. They demonstrate that they are part of the team working towards the shared vision, fostering a sense of unity and mutual respect.

Overall, the concept of 'Erotic Leadership as a Strategy for Success' presents a compelling, holistic approach to leadership that, while less trodden, holds immense potential for driving business success. It acknowledges and harnesses the emotional, passionate side of human nature, creating a more engaged, motivated, and high-performing team.

Talent Management from a Sensual Perspective

Within the realm of talent management, traditional strategies have tended to prioritize easily measurable, tangible attributes. Hiring processes have often focused on candidates' hard skills, specific learned knowledge, and industry expertise, and indeed, such metrics have proven instrumental in constructing successful teams and companies.

Yet, as societal norms evolve and the nature of work transforms in the 21st century, it becomes increasingly apparent that such metrics, while undeniably important, only capture part of the picture. They fail to fully encompass the richness and depth of an individual's potential and their capacity to grow and excel within an organization.

This growing awareness invites us to consider a fresh perspective on talent management, one viewed through a sensual lens. It's crucial to clarify what 'sensual' means within this context, as the term often evokes associations with physical sensation and experience. Here, however, we are broadening its scope to include a heightened level of emotional, mental, and holistic awareness. Through this expanded definition, we start to see employees not simply as workers, but as multifaceted beings, each with a diverse array of needs, desires, and motivations.

In discussing a 'sensual perspective' on talent management, we are referring to an approach that leverages our innate understanding of these intricate layers of human complexity. This perspective enables us to delve beneath surface-level competencies and skills, to shed light on elements such as emotional intelligence, empathy, intrinsic motivations, and mental health, all of which play critical roles in the modern workplace.

The concept of sensual intelligence within talent management proposes an intuitive and empathetic way of understanding and addressing the workforce. It emphasizes the importance of acknowledging and responding to the inherent human needs present in any workplace, focusing on the nuanced interplay between an individual's work and personal life, the effects of stress, the search for purpose, and the deep-seated human need for meaningful connections.

Embracing this perspective requires a significant shift in our conventional mindset. It calls for an approach that sees the workplace not just as a site of production, but as a complex and dynamic ecosystem, teeming with interpersonal relationships, opportunities for personal growth, shared objectives, and the collective pursuit of purpose.

By applying this sensual approach to talent management, the aim is to go beyond conventional performance metrics and technical competencies. The goal becomes to unlock the more profound, often untapped potential within individuals, thereby driving not only enhanced performance but also heightened job satisfaction, well-being, and overall organizational growth.

Through this perspective, we gain a more nuanced understanding of individual motivation, team dynamics, and organizational culture, paving the way for an approach to talent management that is as empathetic and intuitive as it is groundbreaking.

Integrating a sensual perspective into talent management means cultivating an environment that fosters individual uniqueness and intrinsic motivation. This approach goes beyond traditional checklists of qualifications and instead considers the individual as a whole. By acknowledging and valuing employees' diverse backgrounds, experiences, and aspirations, we can encourage a more diverse and innovative workspace.

Emotional intelligence, a cornerstone of the sensual approach, plays a critical role in fostering effective communication, teamwork, and leadership. By honing in on the emotional landscape of the workplace, we can better understand the complexities of interpersonal relationships and manage conflicts with greater empathy and understanding. This heightened awareness can also aid in recognizing signs of burnout or stress among employees, allowing timely interventions and support.

Another key component of this sensual approach is the recognition of the importance of work-life balance. As the boundaries between work and personal life become increasingly blurred, especially with the rise of remote work, understanding an employee's personal circumstances becomes crucial.

A sensual approach to talent management recognizes this balance and encourages policies and practices that respect and support employees' personal lives, leading to improved well-being and job satisfaction.

Moreover, recognizing the role of intrinsic motivation in driving performance and productivity is also essential. When employees feel that their work is meaningful and that they are making significant contributions, they are likely to be more engaged and committed. A sensual approach to talent management means tapping into these intrinsic motivations, aligning individual passions with organizational goals, and creating a sense of purpose in the workplace.

Finally, building meaningful relationships at work is an often overlooked aspect of traditional talent management strategies. Yet, the quality of interpersonal relationships can significantly impact job satisfaction, retention, and overall team performance. A sensual approach values these connections, fostering an environment where employees feel seen, heard, and valued.

Through this sensual lens, we begin to see the workplace not just as a setting for achieving organizational goals but as a human-centric space where individual growth, well-being, and interpersonal connections are nurtured. It offers a holistic way forward, centered on the understanding that every individual brings a unique set of qualities, perspectives, and potential that, when acknowledged and nurtured, can lead to extraordinary results.

As we continue to navigate the ever-evolving landscape of work, this sensual approach to talent management stands as a promising and exciting avenue, equipped to meet the unique demands and complexities of the modern workplace.

Defining Sensual Intelligence in Talent Management

In the vast landscape of talent management, the notion of 'sensual intelligence' might at first appear incongruous or even out of place.

However, it's a concept that, upon deeper exploration, can significantly enrich the approach organizations take to nurturing their most valuable resource: their people.

Sensual intelligence, as we define it in the realm of talent management, underscores a profound comprehension and involvement with the complex, individual experiences of employees. This concept, at its core, emphasizes the power of empathy, intuition, and emotional intelligence.

Unlike the objective, number-driven analyses often used in traditional talent management strategies, this lens focuses on the more nebulous, intangible aspects of an employee's professional life.

In practice, this entails a deep-seated sensitivity towards employees' motivations, aspirations, values, and overall wellbeing. This is not about prying into personal matters but rather acknowledging and appreciating that every individual brings their own unique blend of experiences, ambitions, and personal values to their role.

These elements can significantly influence not only how a person performs in their role but also how they interact with colleagues, react to organizational changes, and engage with their work on a day-to-day basis.

Empathy is an essential component of sensual intelligence. It goes beyond merely understanding an employee's position or situation - it is about genuinely sharing in their feelings and experiences. By fostering an empathetic environment, organizations can establish a space where employees feel seen, heard, and, most importantly, understood.

This can encourage open dialogue, promote trust and respect, and ultimately create a stronger sense of community within the workplace.

Another critical facet of sensual intelligence is intuition. This involves tapping into a more instinctual, gut-level understanding of people and situations. While data and metrics have their place in talent management, they can sometimes fall short of capturing the full picture. Intuition can often bridge this gap, providing valuable insights that aren't immediately apparent from a spreadsheet or a performance review.

A key to effectively implementing sensual intelligence in talent management is to view it as a continuous journey rather than a box-ticking exercise. It involves continually listening, learning, and adjusting approaches based on what is being understood about individual employees and the team as a whole.

Incorporating sensual intelligence into talent management shifts the focus from a standardized, one-size-fits-all approach to a more personalized, tailored strategy. By recognizing and validating the complex array of experiences, emotions, and motivations that each employee brings, organizations can engage with their workforce in a more meaningful, human-centric way. This approach values the individual as a whole person, not just for the skills they bring to the role.

Ultimately, sensual intelligence provides a comprehensive framework for understanding and nurturing the human element within an organization. It pushes the boundaries of traditional talent management, urging us to look beyond quantitative metrics and to embrace the complex, intricate, and wonderfully human aspects of the workforce.

By doing so, organizations not only stand to enhance the job satisfaction and wellbeing of their employees but also to foster a more dynamic, engaged, and motivated workforce, fueling long-term success and growth.

Measuring Sensual Intelligence: The Sensual Intelligence Index

Measuring sensual intelligence, like measuring any form of emotional intelligence, requires a nuanced approach that encompasses both qualitative and quantitative methods. It also involves a keen understanding that sensual intelligence does not exist in a vacuum - it interacts with other traits, skills, and attributes, and thus its measurement needs to take a holistic view. Here are some ways organizations can measure sensual intelligence.

Firstly, it's critical to recognize that sensual intelligence is more about behaviors and attitudes than strictly defined competencies. Observations and feedback on these behaviors can offer valuable insights. Managers and HR professionals might watch for empathy in communication, sensitivity to others' needs and emotions, adaptability in changing circumstances, and the capacity for intuitive decision-making. These signs can indicate a higher level of sensual intelligence.

Self-assessments and 360-degree feedback can be invaluable tools in measuring sensual intelligence. Self-assessments allow individuals to reflect on their own behaviors, motivations, and emotional responses, giving insight into their self-perception of sensual intelligence.

Meanwhile, 360-degree feedback offers a well-rounded view of how an individual's sensual intelligence manifests in their interactions with others, as it incorporates perspectives from peers, supervisors, subordinates, and sometimes even clients.

Structured interviews can also be utilized to gauge sensual intelligence. By posing scenario-based questions, interviewers can explore how individuals might intuitively respond to different situations, offering clues to their sensual intelligence. For instance, a question might ask how they have previously navigated a situation where a colleague was struggling emotionally, or how they've used their intuition to make a decision when data was lacking.

Psychometric tests, specifically designed to measure emotional intelligence and empathy, can be adapted to assess sensual intelligence. While these won't capture all elements of sensual intelligence, they can offer a quantifiable measure that complements the more qualitative methods.

Additionally, measurements of sensual intelligence should be continuously reassessed. As individuals grow and change, so too can their sensual intelligence. Regular check-ins, feedback sessions, and reassessments can help track this growth and change, providing a more accurate and up-to-date understanding of an individual's sensual intelligence.

However, it's vital to remember that while measuring sensual intelligence can offer valuable insights, it shouldn't be used to label or pigeonhole employees. Instead, it should be used to better understand and support individuals, fostering an environment that values and nurtures the human aspect of work.

Concluding on the measure of Sensual Intelligence, it's evident that this multi-faceted concept requires a comprehensive, dynamic, and continuous evaluation strategy. Employing tools such as behavioral observations, self-assessments, 360-degree feedback, structured interviews, and customized psychometric tests can all contribute towards quantifying an individual's sensual intelligence. Furthermore, regular reassessments can ensure an up-to-date understanding of this dynamic attribute, and this information should be used to support individuals in a manner that enhances the overall organizational environment.

As for creating a Sensual Intelligence Index (SII), organizations could develop a proprietary tool combining various methods of evaluation mentioned above. The SII could be scored based on several dimensions correlated with sensual intelligence, including empathic communication, adaptability, intuitive decision-making, and sensitivity towards others' emotions.

For instance, each of these dimensions could be scored on a scale, like a 5-point Likert scale, with each point representing a level of proficiency or frequency of certain behaviors. The scores on all dimensions could then be aggregated to give an overall *Sensual Intelligence Index* for the individual.

To consider the complexity and diversity of sensual intelligence, organizations could also consider including qualitative aspects in the SII. For example, they could incorporate feedback or narratives from peers and supervisors, providing a more nuanced and holistic picture of an individual's sensual intelligence.

However, while developing such an index could provide a useful metric, it's essential to remember the inherently subjective nature of sensual intelligence. The SII should be used as a tool for development and understanding, not as a hard-and-fast label or means of ranking employees. Care should be taken to ensure that the use of such an index respects the diversity and individuality of the workforce and promotes a supportive, inclusive workplace environment.

In conclusion, while measuring sensual intelligence and creating a Sensual Intelligence Index pose unique challenges due to the subjective and dynamic nature of the concept, they hold immense potential in enhancing our understanding of the workforce. With careful implementation and interpretation, they can support a more empathetic, intuitive, and human-centric approach to talent management.

The Role of Sensual Intelligence in Talent Management

The role of sensual intelligence in talent management is wide-ranging and impactful, effectively bringing about a paradigm shift in how we understand, engage, and nurture talent within organizations.

To start with, sensual intelligence fosters a profound understanding of employee needs. In the conventional view of talent management, employees might be seen primarily as assets or resources to be optimized. However, the lens of sensual intelligence reframes this perspective, encouraging managers to see their teams as unique individuals, each with their distinct set of needs, aspirations, and challenges.

By cultivating active listening skills and empathy, managers can delve into these individual experiences, attaining a more accurate understanding of what truly motivates their team members, the obstacles they encounter, and how to most effectively support them. This deep-seated understanding paves the way for meaningful interventions that can enhance job satisfaction, boost performance, and foster a climate of loyalty that promotes higher retention rates.

Moreover, sensual intelligence serves to heighten employee engagement. Traditional engagement methods might focus on reward systems or career progression opportunities, but a sensual approach adds a crucial, often overlooked layer.

By taking a genuine interest in the holistic wellbeing of employees - their physical and mental health, their work-life balance, their social connections within the workplace, and their personal growth - managers can foster an environment of trust, respect, and loyalty. When employees perceive that their employers truly care about them as individuals, they are likely to feel more valued and invested in the organization. This, in turn, can inspire them to contribute their best efforts, enhancing overall productivity and creating a virtuous cycle of engagement and performance.

Finally, sensual intelligence plays a vital role in facilitating personalized development. In the realm of talent management, there is a growing realization that a 'one size fits all' approach to professional development is far from optimal. People come with different skill sets, learning styles, career aspirations, and personal circumstances.

Sensual intelligence equips managers with the insight to recognize these individual differences and to tailor development plans accordingly. This could involve identifying latent talents that could be nurtured, recognizing potential growth areas that require support, and discovering opportunities for mentorship, job rotation or upskilling that align with the employee's aspirations and strengths.

Such a personalized approach can not only enhance the efficacy of development interventions but also make employees feel recognized, understood, and valued, further boosting engagement and retention.

In essence, sensual intelligence brings to the fore the human aspect in talent management.

It pushes us to see beyond numbers and competencies, to understand the unique human experiences that lie beneath, and to tailor our approaches to honor these individual realities. By doing so, it holds the potential to create more empathetic, engaging, and effective workplaces, where every individual feels valued, understood, and motivated to reach their highest potential.

Seductive Recruitment

In an era where both job seekers and organizations are engaged in a constant, dynamic dance of competitive market exchange, the quest for exceptional talent remains paramount. The lifeblood of any organization lies in the quality of its human capital, those unique individuals who, with their distinctive skills and innovative minds, can drive transformation, increase competitiveness, and ultimately fuel the success of their organizations.

Traditional recruitment methods, once considered effective, are beginning to lose their sheen in a world where candidates have the luxury of being selective about their employment choices. To navigate this shifting landscape, organizations are adopting a fresh, evocative approach: seductive recruitment.

Allow me to clarify any ambiguities surrounding the term 'seductive recruitment'. For some, this term may initially raise eyebrows, conjuring images of crafty, manipulative tactics.

However, it's vital to understand that seductive recruitment is far removed from any semblance of deception or misrepresentation. Instead, it's a thoughtful, meticulously crafted strategy designed to appeal to the complex, deeply held aspirations and desires of prospective employees.

At its core, seductive recruitment is an art of engagement and attraction. It's about crafting a tantalizing, captivating vision of what a professional life within the organization could be like. This goes far beyond the transactional aspects of a job, such as remuneration and designated roles. It's about creating a vivid image of an enriched professional experience, where individuals can realize their potential, achieve their career goals, and find personal fulfillment.

What sets this method apart is its ability to highlight the unique characteristics that make the organization stand out. Each organization has its distinctive facets — the aspects that set it apart from the rest. It could be a nurturing culture that encourages continuous learning and growth, a leadership approach that fosters innovation and creativity, a strong commitment to corporate social responsibility, or a track record of acknowledging and rewarding employee contributions. Through seductive recruitment, these attributes are brought to the fore, painting the organization not just as another workplace, but as a desirable destination for both personal and professional growth.

The result is a powerful, authentic narrative that resonates with potential employees' individual motivations and ambitions. The organization is seen not as a faceless entity, but as a platform that aligns with their values, fuels their passions, and facilitates their career trajectory.

Thus, the essence of seductive recruitment lies not in deceit or manipulation, but in presenting an accurate, enticing image of the organization that speaks to the heart of potential employees' aspirations and desires.

This approach deepens engagement, stirs interest, and ultimately attracts talent who identify strongly with the organization's values and vision. This is the essence of seductive recruitment. Seductive recruitment pivots on understanding what truly attracts potential employees.

This understanding dives much deeper than the surface-level elements of salary and benefits. It encompasses elements like the company's culture, the opportunities it provides for personal and career growth, the organization's mission and values, the balance it offers between work and personal life, and more. Recognizing that every candidate is a unique individual with their own career goals, values, and aspirations, it's paramount for organizations to project an image that resonates with these individual traits and ambitions.

A powerful tool in the seductive recruitment arsenal is storytelling. By weaving a compelling narrative about its culture, values, or the impact it's had, an organization can draw in candidates who find a deep resonance with this story.

The tale could relate to the founding of the company, a significant challenge it surmounted, a project that sparked considerable positive change, or even stories of its employees who have carved out satisfying and rewarding careers within its fold. Storytelling humanizes the organization, transforming it from an abstract entity into a relatable collective, enhancing its appeal to potential employees.

Creating an immersive experience during the recruitment process is another key strategy in seductive recruitment. This could involve extending invitations to candidates to spend a day at the office, meet their potential colleagues, or participate in company activities. Such experiences offer candidates an opportunity to sample the work environment, the culture, and the people they would potentially be collaborating with. This taste of the organization's life can serve to allure them further, building an emotional connection that could sway their decision.

Conversing actively with potential employees constitutes a further critical strategy. This involves not only discussions around job roles and responsibilities, but also explorations into the candidate's career aspirations, personal goals, and values. This engagement provides a platform for the organization to demonstrate how it can facilitate the fulfillment of these aspirations, making the prospect of joining the organization even more enticing.

In today's connected world, social media can play a significant role in seductive recruitment. A vibrant social media presence that showcases the organization's culture, its people, its triumphs, and its values can magnetize candidates who find alignment with these facets. This could involve sharing posts about company events, employee achievements, CSR initiatives, or even casual, behind-the-scenes snapshots of the company's life.

Seductive recruitment, therefore, emerges as a forward-thinking approach to talent acquisition that goes beyond the ordinary. By creating an enticing vision of what working for the organization could be like and presenting an authentic, attractive image of its culture, values, and vision, organizations can lure top talent who find a deep resonance with these attributes. In doing so, they set the stage for a more engaged, motivated, and successful workforce that is bound to drive the organization to greater heights.

Motivating and Retaining Talent through Erotism

Understanding human motivation is key to effective talent management, especially when it comes to retaining top talent in a competitive job market. Over the years, a variety of theories have been proposed to explain what drives us to act the way we do, from Maslow's hierarchy of needs to Herzberg's two-factor theory. Yet, one facet of motivation that has not been extensively explored in the professional context is erotism.

Now, to clarify, the term "erotism" here is not used in its conventional, sexual sense. Rather, it takes inspiration from the philosophical context as used by ancient Greeks where "Eros" was seen as a form of love that transcends the physical and reaches into the realm of mind and spirit. We will explore how the principle of erotism, understood as the pursuit of passion, creativity, and intense human connection, can be used to motivate and retain talent.

Firstly, we start by acknowledging the role of passion in the workplace. The term 'passion', in this context, conveys a deep-seated enthusiasm for one's work, a drive that transcends the mere obligation to perform tasks and extends to a genuine joy found in the process and outcomes of the work itself. This kind of passion is a central element of erotism, representing an intense, absorbing fascination that's vital in fostering a motivated and engaged workforce.

Creating an environment that encourages employees to pursue their passions requires understanding that each employee is an individual with unique interests, skills, and aspirations. Therefore, the key lies in tapping into these unique passions, which requires an open, attentive approach from management. This means not only asking employees what they are passionate about but genuinely listening to their responses and acting upon them where possible.

Granting employees more autonomy in their work can greatly contribute to this. Autonomy allows employees to shape their roles in ways that align with their passions, leading to greater job satisfaction and engagement. This could involve giving them the freedom to approach tasks in ways that they find most fulfilling or allowing them the flexibility to structure their workdays to balance their professional and personal passions.

Furthermore, providing opportunities for professional growth is another vital aspect of fostering passion. This could mean offering training and development programs aligned with employees' interests, providing mentorship opportunities, or encouraging participation in relevant industry events or conferences. When employees see a clear path for growth and advancement that aligns with their passions, they are likely to be more committed to the organization.

Supporting side projects or skills development can also be a powerful way to encourage passion. This could involve providing resources or time for employees to pursue projects related to their interests, even if they fall outside their formal job descriptions. For example, Google's famous "20% time" policy allows employees to spend 20% of their time working on any project they choose, leading to innovations like Gmail and Google News.

In a broader sense, promoting passion in the workplace also requires creating a culture that values and celebrates enthusiasm, creativity, and dedication. This means recognizing and rewarding passionate work, promoting success stories, and ensuring that passion is reflected in the organization's values and mission.

Diving deeper into this notion, we must acknowledge that creativity stands at the heart of erotism. Both creativity and erotism share a deep connection with novelty, experimentation, and a drive to transcend ordinary boundaries. Just as erotism seeks to push the boundaries of intensity and emotional depth, creativity aims to breach the confines of conventional thinking and venture into new intellectual territories.

In an organizational context, a work environment that actively encourages creativity is not merely a space where new ideas are welcomed; it's an arena where original thinking is anticipated, respected, and rewarded.

It becomes fertile ground for employees to fully express their intellectual curiosity, to challenge the status quo, and to weave their unique perspectives into the fabric of the organization's future. When employees feel that their creativity is valued, they are likely to feel a stronger sense of attachment to their work and, by extension, to the organization itself.

Yet, fostering a creative environment isn't as simple as making a declaration; it involves building a culture. A culture that doesn't fear risk-taking but embraces it as a necessary steppingstone towards innovation. This is where the concept of erotism further intertwines with creativity. Erotism embodies a willingness to explore, to venture into the unknown, and to take risks – qualities that are intrinsic to creative thinking.

Organizations that promote a growth mindset, viewing challenges and setbacks as fuel for learning rather than as detriments, send a clear message to their employees: creativity is not just about successes, but about the lessons learned in the journey. This perspective reframes failure, a concept often feared and avoided, into a valuable opportunity for growth and learning. In this environment, employees are more likely to take creative risks, secure in the knowledge that their efforts will be valued, even if they don't always lead to immediate success.

The celebration of creativity also involves tangible recognition of creative efforts. Whether through rewards, acknowledgments, or simply through the implementation of new ideas, recognizing creativity further enhances its value within the organization. When employees see their creative contributions influencing their workplace, their sense of belonging and commitment intensifies. Finally, erotism is about intense human connection, which translates into the workplace as strong, authentic relationships among team members.

Building a supportive community within the organization, where employees feel seen, heard, and appreciated, can significantly increase their commitment to the organization. This could involve regular team-building activities, open and honest communication, recognition of individual achievements, and support during challenging times.

Furthermore, this sense of connection should extend to the relationship between employees and the organization itself. This means that the organization needs to demonstrate that it values its employees not just as workers, but as people, for example by taking an interest in their wellbeing, respecting their work-life balance, and responding to their feedback.

Implementing these principles of erotism in the workplace is not a quick fix. It requires a shift in organizational culture, and a commitment to value employees as complex, creative individuals with their own passions and goals.

However, by creating a work environment that nurtures passion, creativity, and human connection, organizations can significantly enhance their ability to motivate and retain top talent.

It's about moving beyond the transactional, and embracing the full, rich potential of human experience at work. It's not just about making work more enjoyable; it's about making it more meaningful, more fulfilling, and ultimately, more erotic.

Continuing with the essence of the erotic in the workplace, it's essential to acknowledge the role of leadership in fostering such an environment. Leaders are instrumental in setting the tone and culture of an organization. When leaders demonstrate passion for their work, value creativity, and foster authentic connections, these attitudes can permeate the entire organization.

In this sense, the principle of erotism should not be confined to specific teams or departments but should become part of the overall organizational ethos.

Leaders can incorporate the principles of erotism in various ways. For instance, they can inspire passion by clearly communicating the organization's vision and values, highlighting how each role contributes to the larger goals.

They can foster creativity by welcoming diverse perspectives, promoting innovative thinking, and encouraging risk-taking. They can nurture human connections by demonstrating empathy, showing genuine interest in their team members as individuals, and promoting a culture of collaboration and mutual respect.

However, these principles require not only inspiration but also dedication. Change doesn't happen overnight, and it's important to acknowledge that this transformation will require effort, time, and patience.

Organizations may need to reassess their current practices, address potential obstacles, and perhaps most importantly, be willing to learn and adapt along the way. Yet the rewards, in terms of increased employee motivation, job satisfaction, and talent retention, can be substantial.

Importantly, the principle of erotism goes beyond mere employee retention and motivation. It presents a broader perspective on the very purpose and nature of work. It challenges the traditional, transactional view of employment as merely a means to an end, and instead, positions work as a potential source of passion, creativity, and deep human connection.

In this light, work becomes not just a duty, but an expression of one's interests, talents, and values. It's about finding pleasure and fulfillment in the work we do and the contributions we make.

Navigating deeper into this conclusion, we find that the introduction of erotism as a fundamental principle in talent management holds an intriguing potential to reshape how organizations understand and respond to their employees' intrinsic needs and desires.

The concept of erotism, here, does not carry its conventional sensual connotation. Instead, it reflects a deeper, more nuanced understanding of human passion, enthusiasm, and the desire for meaningful connections and experiences.

Central to the idea of erotism in talent management is the belief that work should not merely be a platform for transactions but a space for personal and professional fulfillment.

This perspective propels us beyond the traditional parameters of motivation and retention. It impels us to focus on passion, the kind of raw, unfiltered enthusiasm that drives employees to commit to their roles not merely because they have to, but because they truly want to.

When employees can align their passions with their work, their professional pursuits transform into personal quests, imbued with a sense of purpose that transcends contractual obligations.

In the same vein, the nurturing of creativity in the workplace serves as another cornerstone of this erotic-centric approach. When creativity is valued and rewarded, employees feel free to express their unique perspectives, push boundaries, and generate new ideas. They become active contributors to the organization's growth rather than passive participants.

The culture of creativity creates a landscape where employees can continually reinvent their relationship with their work, ensuring a sustained level of engagement that goes beyond the monotonous routine. This continuous exploration and reinvention are inherently erotic, reflecting a zest for novel experiences.

Moreover, the role of human connection in erotism-based talent management is not to be underestimated. Employees are likely to be more committed and motivated when they feel genuinely connected to their peers, their managers, and the organization itself. This connectivity derives not only from professional interactions but also from shared values, common goals, and mutual respect. It promotes a sense of belonging that can significantly enhance employee retention.

Therefore, by adopting an approach rooted in erotism, organizations can stimulate a more profound level of engagement among their employees. This isn't a superficial, fleeting engagement derived from transient rewards, but a sustained, deeply rooted commitment born out of passion, creativity, and connection.

In effect, by incorporating the principles of erotism into their talent management strategies, organizations can revolutionize not just how they motivate and retain talent, but also how work is perceived and experienced by their employees. The workplace thus becomes a platform for self-expression, growth, and fulfillment.

In essence, this approach transforms work from a mundane obligation into an exciting, satisfying, and indeed, a decidedly more erotic adventure. It's an innovative step towards a future where work can be as much about personal satisfaction and growth as it is about professional success.

Enhancing Professional Development with Erotic Elements

A Paradigm Shift in Talent Growth

Professional development has long been understood as an integral aspect of career progression, traditionally approached via formal training, workshops, and courses aimed at building technical competencies and industry-specific knowledge. However, this standard approach, while still essential, has come under scrutiny for its potential disconnect with the more complex, nuanced facets of human growth.

A nascent perspective gaining momentum in progressive HR circles advocates for a more radical approach: enhancing professional development with erotic elements.

As we have mentioned in previous section on this book, the term 'erotic' here does not allude to anything sexual. Instead, it is used in the broader, metaphorical sense derived from the ancient Greek concept of 'Eros', representing desire, passion, and love. This concept reaches beyond the mere acquisition of skills into a space where learning, creativity, and growth are driven by deeper human desires, passions, and connections. Thus, incorporating 'erotic' elements into professional development necessitates an exploration of these deeper, often overlooked aspects of professional growth.

Passion forms the cornerstone of this erotic perspective on professional development. It is the fuel that powers the human spirit, the driving force that can lead to profound commitment and extraordinary achievements.

Therefore, aligning professional development initiatives with an individual's passions can profoundly boost engagement, satisfaction, and effectiveness. This could manifest as opportunities for employees to pursue projects tied to their interests or involve their passions within their tasks, making their professional journey more personally resonant and fulfilling.

Creativity, another crucial element, holds transformative power within the sphere of professional development. Creativity drives innovation, problem-solving, and fosters a more nuanced understanding of work, making it a key erotic element. Encouraging creative thought processes and exploration can invigorate professional development, making it a dynamic, intellectually stimulating process rather than a rote, checklist-driven task. It offers an environment where unique ideas are valued, where failures are seen as opportunities for learning and growth, and where individuals are motivated to think beyond the conventional, fostering a fertile ground for personal and professional evolution.

Human connection, a deeply erotic element, also plays a pivotal role in this alternative perspective on professional development. The power of authentic, meaningful relationships in the workspace extends beyond networking or collaboration.

It enhances empathy, promotes diversity of thought, and fosters an environment conducive to mentorship and knowledge sharing. The sense of belonging, alignment with organizational values, and the mutual investment in shared goals that arises from genuine connections in the workplace can significantly amplify the effectiveness of professional development programs.

Introspection forms a crucial facet of the erotic approach to professional development. It involves an inward journey, a process of self-reflection that encourages individuals to look beyond their surface-level competencies to explore their deeper, inner world. This journey can unlock profound insights into one's intrinsic motivations, aspirations, strengths, and areas that need growth or improvement, making it a potent tool for personal and professional development.

By turning our gaze inward, we can start to understand what truly drives us, what genuinely ignites our passion. These are not merely the ambitions that society, our families, or our peers have laid out for us but are derived from our own deeply held desires and interests. Understanding these intrinsic motivations is key to fostering a sense of purpose and fulfillment in our work. It helps align our professional path with our personal desires, resulting in greater job satisfaction, engagement, and productivity.

Similarly, introspection can shed light on our unique strengths, those qualities or skills that set us apart. In the corporate world, where comparison is rife, it's easy to undervalue our strengths, especially when they don't align with traditionally recognized or sought-after skills. However, by recognizing and appreciating our unique capabilities, we can leverage them to our advantage, carving out a niche for ourselves and contributing to our organizations in distinctive, meaningful ways.

Introspection also plays a critical role in identifying areas for improvement. By acknowledging our shortcomings without judgment, we can adopt a proactive approach to personal and professional development. We can seek out opportunities to learn, grow, and challenge ourselves, transforming perceived weaknesses into new strengths. This process is not only beneficial for career progression but also promotes personal growth and resilience.

Moreover, introspection fosters a deeper level of self-understanding, an awareness that extends beyond the professional sphere into personal realms. It nurtures a sense of self-compassion, self-respect, and self-love, crucial components for mental well-being. By knowing ourselves better, we can navigate professional challenges with greater clarity, make career decisions more aligned with our values, and establish healthier work-life boundaries.

On the organizational level, promoting a culture that values introspection can yield considerable benefits. It can lead to a more engaged, self-aware workforce, fostering a sense of ownership, independence, and self-driven growth among employees. It encourages an environment where individuals are seen and valued for who they are, not just for their professional competencies, thereby enhancing job satisfaction, loyalty, and overall organizational culture.

In essence, introspection stands as a profoundly significant component of the erotic approach to professional development. By embracing a culture of self-reflection and self-understanding, individuals and organizations can nurture a more meaningful, human-centric approach to growth and development.

This depth of awareness and understanding not only paves the way for more personalized and effective professional development but also promotes personal growth, fulfillment, and a deeper understanding of one's self.

As we bring this discussion to a close, it is evident that the incorporation of erotic elements into professional development breathes new life into traditionally monotonous, transactional processes.

By embracing the principles of passion, creativity, authenticity, and introspection, professional development shifts from being merely a series of boxes to be checked in the pursuit of career advancement to a multi-dimensional journey of personal and professional growth and fulfillment.

At its core, professional development should be a deeply personal journey. It should reflect an individual's desires, motivations, and interests. This is where the role of passion becomes paramount. By cultivating an environment where employees are encouraged to pursue their passions, organizations allow their workforce to fully engage in their work. The result? A highly motivated, satisfied team that brings its whole self to the job, igniting a powerful cycle of engagement, productivity, and retention.

Creativity, another cornerstone of erotism, is equally critical in this new paradigm. A work environment that encourages creativity values innovation, embraces new ideas, and fosters a culture of risk-taking.

This not only enables employees to contribute in unique and valuable ways, but also instills a sense of ownership and pride in their work.

In this environment, professional development becomes a process of constant learning, adaptation, and evolution.

In the realm of authenticity, erotism underlines the importance of forming genuine, human connections in the workplace. When employees feel genuinely connected to their colleagues, their managers, and the organization's mission, they are likely to be more committed and engaged. Authentic relationships also create a supportive, collaborative atmosphere, fostering a culture of shared learning and mutual professional development.

Introspection, as discussed, acts as the bedrock of this erotic approach to professional development. It encourages individuals to look inward, to reflect upon their intrinsic motivations, their unique strengths, and their areas for improvement.

This process of self-discovery and self-understanding paves the way for a more personalized, meaningful journey of professional development.

In conclusion, the integration of erotic elements offers a radical reimagining of professional development.

It moves away from a one-dimensional, transactional model to a holistic, human-centric approach that values passion, creativity, authentic connections, and introspection.

This model sees professional development not as a mandatory career task, but as an enriching path of personal and professional fulfillment, a journey that fosters a more engaged, satisfied, and successful workforce.

This shift towards an erotic perspective on professional development represents a paradigm shift in our understanding of meaningful, holistic growth within the professional sphere.

It calls on us to reevaluate and redefine how we approach professional development, offering a framework that is as profoundly human as it is revolutionary.

Success, Power, and Attraction

The interplay between success, power, and attraction has long been a topic of interest in various fields, from psychology and sociology to business and leadership studies. Understanding the intricate relationship between these three aspects can provide insights into human behavior, organizational dynamics, and societal structures.

The intersection of success, power, and attraction is a complex matrix that shapes individual behaviors, societal values, and the way we interact with the world around us. All three concepts are not static but are malleable and are influenced by personal beliefs, societal norms, and historical contexts.

In the context of success, it is primarily seen as a measure of achievement, an assessment of one's abilities, skills, or circumstances. Success, whether personal or professional, is generally perceived as the result of hard work, intelligence, or inherent talent. However, the definition of success can vary greatly among individuals, cultures, and societies. For example, while some may view success as attaining a high-ranking position in a corporation, others might define success as leading a balanced and fulfilling life.

In essence, success is a validation of one's efforts and abilities. But what often goes overlooked is the role power and attraction play in shaping this success. Power, whether it's social, political, or economic, can provide opportunities and access to resources that might make the path to success smoother. Similarly, attraction, be it personal charisma, the appeal of a particular job or company, or the allure of specific ideas or goals, can often act as a catalyst, fueling the desire to pursue success.

Power, as a concept, extends beyond the basic ability to control or influence others. It includes the ability to shape narratives, impact decisions, and drive change on a larger scale. Power isn't always tied to formal roles or positions. Informal power sources, such as knowledge, charisma, or moral authority, can be equally potent. Power, when used responsibly, can lead to positive change, facilitate progress, and enable success. However, it can also breed inequality and injustice if misused or unchecked.

Attraction, meanwhile, influences the choices we make and the paths we follow. It's about what draws us in, be it a person, idea, or goal. Attraction can be intellectual, emotional, or physical, often guiding our decisions, shaping our pursuits, and impacting our concept of success. For example, the attraction to certain values or principles can motivate us to pursue careers in public service or social activism. Similarly, attraction towards wealth and status might lead others towards high-powered jobs in finance or technology.

At the convergence of success, power, and attraction lie some of society's most compelling impetuses. These multifaceted constructs, though individually influential, form an intricate, often synergistic matrix that propels individuals' actions, sculpt societal trajectories, and underpin cultural norms.

By discerning this dynamic, we equip ourselves with the knowledge to better manage our personal and professional endeavors, to analyze critically the societal structures and norms that envelop us, and to understand the forces shaping the world.

The relationship between success and power is indeed complex and frequently symbiotic, forming a feedback loop of mutual reinforcement. Success, particularly in a professional domain, often paves the way to power. This power may manifest as authority over others, as the capacity to sway or influence, or as control over resources or decision-making processes. Achieving a high-ranking position, for instance, not only signifies career success but also imbues an individual with authority and influence within the organization. Winning a prestigious award in a specific field might confer an individual with power in the form of respect and recognition, further amplifying their capacity to succeed.

Conversely, those who possess power, either through their role, knowledge, or network, often have a head start on the path to success. Power can open doors to opportunities, grant access to vital resources, and facilitate decision-making autonomy—all critical components for achieving success.

For example, a business leader with expansive industry connections (a form of power) can leverage these relationships to create opportunities for business growth, contributing to their personal and organizational success.

However, it is crucial to recognize that this relationship between success and power is not always equitable or fair. In many instances, societal structures can privilege certain individuals, enabling them to gain power and achieve success more easily than others. Thus, it is imperative to critically examine these constructs not just in isolation, but in the broader context of societal inequalities and systemic biases.

At the same time, attraction serves as a significant factor within this dynamic triad. It is the gravitational pull that directs our choices, aligning our decisions with our desires. Attraction, whether it's to an individual, a career path, a lifestyle, or a set of values, forms the basis of our aspirations, which in turn shape our measures of success. In addition, the attractiveness of power and success can motivate individuals to pursue specific paths, further reinforcing the interconnected nature of these three constructs. Attraction plays a critical role in this dynamic.

The allure of success and power can be quite potent. Individuals who embody success often hold an array of captivating qualities or resources. This can range from exuding self-assurance and holding financial security to possessing distinctive skills and noteworthy attributes. All these factors can elevate their attractiveness in various contexts.

In a similar vein, power, too, has an undeniable appeal. Those with the ability to sway others, whether through direct control or influence, tend to elicit a certain level of respect, admiration, and at times, awe. The magnetism of power resides not just in the authority it holds, but also in the potential for impact and change that it represents.

However, the role of attraction extends beyond being a mere consequence of success and power. It fundamentally influences the attainment of both. In the realm of professional pursuits, the allure of certain individuals, stemming from their skills, knowledge, or a myriad of other qualities, greatly enhances their prospects for success. Their attractiveness in this regard can make them favorable candidates for hiring or promotions, providing them with greater opportunities for advancement.

The concept of attractiveness also extends to organizations and even ideas. Those entities that can evoke interest or align with people's values have the potential to amass substantial power. They can guide decision-making, shape prevailing narratives, or galvanize support.

For instance, an organization with a compelling mission and value proposition can attract top talent, fostering a powerful workforce. Similarly, an attractive idea, be it a social movement or a technological innovation, can sway public opinion, shift paradigms, and mobilize collective action.

In this context, attractiveness is not just about physical appeal but encompasses a wide spectrum of traits, capabilities, and values. Recognizing the reciprocal relationship between attractiveness, success, and power can lead to a more nuanced understanding of their interplay, aiding individuals and organizations in their pursuit of these objectives. By nurturing and showcasing attractive qualities, individuals and entities can enhance their potential for success and influence, ultimately magnifying their impact in the world.

Yet, it's crucial to recognize that success, power, and attraction are not inherently positive or negative. Their value and impact largely depend on how they are pursued and utilized. Success pursued at the expense of others can lead to dissatisfaction and conflict. Power wielded without regard for ethics can lead to injustice and resentment. Attraction based on superficial or manipulative grounds can lead to shallow relationships and mistrust.

In essence, the dynamic interplay between success, power, and attraction choreographs a complex performance that deeply influences the trajectory of our lives. This intricate relationship not only shapes our aspirations and actions but also significantly impacts our societal structures and cultural norms.

By decoding this intricate dynamic, we equip ourselves with deeper insights that can illuminate our personal and professional paths, enabling us to navigate life's many stages with more wisdom and purposefulness.

Embracing this understanding can empower us to pursue a brand of success that extends beyond material accomplishments and societal accolades. It can encourage us to seek out success that is enriching and personally fulfilling, one that aligns with our authentic selves and core values. Rather than conforming to generic benchmarks, we can redefine success on our own terms, considering aspects such as personal growth, happiness, balance, and meaningful contributions to society.

Furthermore, this understanding can guide us in wielding power responsibly and ethically. Power, when tempered with empathy, wisdom, and a commitment to fairness, can be an influential force for good. We can strive to utilize power not as a means to dominate or control, but as a tool to create positive change, inspire others, and uphold justice and equality. Power, then, becomes not an end in itself, but a means to foster an environment of collaboration, respect, and mutual growth.

To sum it up, the complex interweaving of success, power, and attraction forms a rich tapestry that shapes our lives, societies, and cultures in myriad ways. By exploring and understanding these threads, we can navigate our personal and professional landscapes with more consciousness and intention.

This insight allows us to cultivate a fulfilling success, ethically utilized power, and attraction based on substantive and authentic qualities, ultimately fostering a more compassionate, equitable, and meaningful world.

The Impact of Success on Attraction in the context of Erotism in Management

Erotism in Management is a concept that explores how elements of erotic or sexual attraction manifest and influence dynamics within the workplace.

Unlike Erotic Management, which focuses on the strategic use of sexuality or sexual attractiveness, Erotism in Management takes a broader view, examining how sexual attraction, in general, shapes relationships, decision-making, and power dynamics within a professional setting.

Erotism in Management involves understanding and acknowledging the undercurrents of human desires and attraction that inherently exist within the shared spaces of the workplace.

Recognizing the role of these undercurrents can shed light on certain behaviors and tendencies that may otherwise remain obscured or misunderstood. For instance, interpersonal dynamics, communication styles, conflict resolution mechanisms, and team bonding exercises may all be influenced, subtly or overtly, by elements of erotism.

Attraction, as a fundamental aspect of human interaction, naturally permeates the professional environment as well. How individuals react to this attraction, navigate it, and potentially utilize it, forms the basis of understanding Erotism in Management. It extends beyond merely physical attraction, encompassing the full range of emotional, intellectual, and even spiritual dimensions that contribute to our connection with others.

The dynamics of attraction can often significantly impact decision-making within an organization. It may unconsciously bias the allocation of resources, assignments, promotions, or opportunities towards those individuals deemed more attractive, charismatic, or compelling.

Understanding and accounting for these biases is crucial in promoting fairness, equality, and integrity within the workplace.

Power dynamics within a professional setting may also be influenced by elements of erotism. An individual's ability to command attention, inspire, persuade, or lead could be enhanced or impeded by these dynamics. In some instances, these dynamics can foster positive outcomes, such as increased confidence, motivation, or unity within a team. However, if misused or left unchecked, they could also lead to harmful consequences such as favoritism, discrimination, or exploitation.

Therefore, leaders and managers must be mindful and sensitive when navigating Erotism in Management. A delicate balance must be struck to harness the positive aspects of these dynamics, such as enhancing interpersonal relationships or fostering a vibrant and engaging work environment, while mitigating potential negative impacts. It is essential to ensure a culture of respect and professionalism, where boundaries are clearly established and maintained, and where all interactions are guided by principles of consent and equality.

Furthermore, educating employees about these dynamics can help create a more transparent, understanding, and empathetic workplace. Providing training and resources to help individuals recognize and manage the impact of erotism on their professional interactions can empower them to navigate these dynamics effectively and ethically.

Ultimately, the concept of Erotism in Management encourages a more holistic understanding of the workplace, one that accounts for the complex and multifaceted nature of human interactions. It invites us to acknowledge and embrace the role of attraction within professional settings while ensuring a culture of respect, consent, and fairness. By doing so, organizations can foster a more inclusive, engaging, and balanced work environment, enhancing both individual satisfaction and collective productivity.

Now, let's delve into the impact of success on attraction within this particular context:

Enhanced Attraction Through Success:

The phenomenon of Enhanced Attraction Through Success plays a crucial role in shaping the dynamics of a professional environment. Success, whether manifested through individual achievement, positional power, or professional recognition, can significantly magnify an individual's appeal.

This attraction extends beyond physical attributes, permeating aspects of character, personality, and capability, often making successful individuals highly influential within their professional circles.

The personal attraction stemming from individual traits is often amplified in the face of success. Traits such as confidence, competence, and charm become more pronounced and appealing when coupled with tangible accomplishments. This magnetism can create an aura of leadership, making successful individuals' natural influencers, motivators, and decision-makers within a team or organization.

Simultaneously, professional attraction derived from status, influence, or recognition also grows with success. An individual who attains a high-status role, wields significant influence, or gains wide recognition often becomes a beacon of admiration, respect, and, in some cases, emulation. This enhanced attraction can fortify their authority, foster trust and loyalty, and inspire others to strive for similar achievements.

However, Enhanced Attraction Through Success can have multifaceted implications in a workplace setting. On one hand, it can serve as a driving force that propels teamwork, boosts morale, and cultivates a culture of excellence. Employees might feel more engaged and motivated when working with individuals they admire or aspire to emulate. It can also foster healthy competition, driving individuals to improve their skills and performance.

On the other hand, the potent influence exerted by highly successful individuals can potentially skew decision-making processes and disrupt objectivity. It might lead to situations where ideas, opinions, or decisions are accepted without adequate scrutiny simply because they originate from a highly attractive and successful individual.

Moreover, the presence of strong attraction can risk the emergence of favoritism, discrimination, or even harassment. Hence, while Enhanced Attraction Through Success can be a powerful tool in fostering a motivated and aspirational work environment, it must be handled with responsibility, fairness, and a clear understanding of ethical boundaries.

The concept of Enhanced Attraction Through Success, thus, is a critical component of Erotism in Management. It helps us comprehend how success shapes and influences the magnetic appeal of individuals within the workplace, consequently impacting interpersonal dynamics, decision-making processes, and power structures. Recognizing and navigating this enhanced attraction judiciously can contribute to creating a balanced, equitable, and highly motivated work environment.

Success as a Marker of Attractiveness:

The notion of Success as a Marker of Attractiveness provides a compelling perspective on how professional achievement influences interpersonal dynamics within the workplace. Success often manifests itself as a proxy for various desirable attributes, making individuals with notable achievements highly appealing to their peers, subordinates, and superiors.

When individuals achieve success, they showcase a spectrum of qualities that are highly valued in the professional sphere. These qualities might include intelligence, exemplified by problem-solving skills or innovative thinking; ambition, indicated by goal-orientation and tenacity; persistence, demonstrated by resilience in the face of challenges; and resourcefulness, shown through effective use of available resources or creative approach towards problem-solving.

The presence of these attributes paints a picture of a competent, driven, and capable individual. As a result, successful individuals often command respect, admiration, and attraction from others in their professional circle. This elevated status of attractiveness can subsequently influence a range of interpersonal dynamics within the workplace.

For instance, employees might be more inclined to associate with, learn from, or seek guidance from colleagues who have demonstrated success. Similarly, managers might favor successful employees with more responsibilities, opportunities, or rewards, banking on their proven ability to deliver positive results. Moreover, successful individuals might enjoy greater influence in team discussions or organizational decisions, owing to the perceived wisdom and competence attached to their success.

However, viewing Success as a Marker of Attractiveness also necessitates careful consideration of potential pitfalls. The enhanced appeal of successful individuals might lead to bias or preferential treatment, potentially creating an imbalance in the workplace. It could inadvertently sideline other employees who might have valuable contributions to make but haven't had the opportunity to demonstrate notable success yet.

Moreover, equating success with attractiveness might create a high-pressure environment where employees feel compelled to constantly achieve in order to gain recognition and acceptance. It's essential for organizations to balance the admiration for success with an understanding and acknowledgment of effort, growth, and potential.

Therefore, the concept of Success as a Marker of Attractiveness, while instrumental in shaping workplace dynamics, must be contextualized within a broader framework of equity, inclusivity, and respect for diverse paths to success. By doing so, organizations can cultivate a culture that values success, while also nurturing the multifaceted potential of all its members.

Power and Influence Dynamics:

The intertwining relationship between success, power, influence, and attractiveness paints a vivid picture of the complexity of professional dynamics within an organization. As individuals ascend the ladder of success, they invariably accumulate a degree of power and influence, contributing to their perceived attractiveness within the workplace.

This heightened attractiveness often operates as a subtle undercurrent, subtly steering the course of decisions, negotiations, and relationships.

A successful individual, adorned with the mantles of power and influence, commands a unique position within the professional ecosystem. They are often seen as role models, their opinions are given more weight, and their actions can set precedents for others to follow. Whether consciously or unconsciously, these individuals can use their attractiveness as a tool to shape and guide workplace dynamics.

For instance, they might leverage their attractiveness to influence the decision-making process, nudging it in directions that align with their own perspectives or interests. This can have a significant impact on everything from day-to-day operations to long-term strategic planning. Given their appealing persona, they often find it easier to rally support for their ideas, ensuring their vision becomes a shared reality for the team or the organization.

Similarly, in the realm of negotiations, these individuals can utilize their attractiveness to sway outcomes in their favor. Whether it's securing a lucrative deal, obtaining favorable terms in a contract, or negotiating a promotion or a raise, their success-enhanced attractiveness often provides them with a distinct advantage.

Furthermore, the attractiveness derived from power and success can shape interpersonal relationships within the workplace. It can foster alliances, instigate rivalries, and inspire mentorships. Employees might strive to forge strong relationships with these individuals, seeking to learn from their success, gain their endorsement, or align themselves with the power they hold.

However, it is important to understand that while these dynamics can stimulate a competitive and high-performing environment, they may also introduce challenges. The concentration of power and influence in certain individuals might inadvertently create a hierarchical and polarized work culture. There could be a risk of these individuals monopolizing dialogues, overshadowing other voices, or fostering a culture of favoritism.

Additionally, the pressure to maintain their attractive status might lead successful individuals to make choices that prioritize their personal success over the collective good of the organization. Hence, it is essential to create checks and balances that prevent the misuse of power, and foster a culture of shared leadership where influence is distributed and everyone's contribution is valued.

Role of Success in Shaping Perception:

Success can also shape perception in a way that magnifies attractiveness. This is related to the psychological concept known as the "halo effect", where an individual's positive qualities (such as success) can lead others to perceive them as more attractive overall. In a workplace setting, this could mean that successful individuals are viewed as more competent, charismatic, or influential, adding a layer of complexity to the dynamics of Erotism in Management.

Sociocultural Factors: Success's impact on attraction can also be influenced by sociocultural factors. Different societies and cultures have various definitions and measures of success and attractiveness.

For example, some cultures might value financial success and stability, enhancing the attractiveness of individuals who embody these qualities. On the other hand, other cultures might place more emphasis on social connections or personal attributes, which could likewise influence perceptions of attractiveness within the workplace.

While understanding the intersection of success and attraction in the context of Erotism in Management is crucial, it's also important to consider the potential challenges and ethical implications. For instance, the dynamics of attraction and success can sometimes lead to favoritism, bias, or even harassment within the workplace.

Therefore, organizations must strive to cultivate an environment that values professionalism, respect, and equality, recognizing and addressing the potential issues that can arise from the interplay of success and attraction.

In essence, the influence of success on attraction, when viewed through the lens of Erotism in Management, is an intricate and multi-dimensional dynamic. It isn't a simple one-way street; rather, it resembles an elaborate dance that is shaped by a plethora of factors, including personal traits, professional accomplishments, power dynamics, and sociocultural norms. Each component interacts with and influences the others, thereby adding layers of complexity to this already intricate dance.

This dance necessitates a high level of awareness and understanding from all participants. Individuals, regardless of their level of success, need to be mindful of how their behaviors and attitudes can be influenced by, and in turn, influence, the dynamics of attraction within the workplace. This might mean examining their own biases, re-evaluating their perceptions of others, or being more conscious of how they wield their influence.

Organizations, too, play a critical role in navigating this dance. They must cultivate an environment that respects the complexity of these dynamics while prioritizing fairness and equity.

This could involve implementing robust policies to prevent and address issues like favoritism, bias, and harassment. It might also mean encouraging open dialogue about these issues, providing training to employees, or investing in diversity and inclusion initiatives.

Moreover, the concept of success itself needs to be understood more broadly. Beyond financial gains or professional growth, success can also encompass personal development, ethical conduct, and contributions to a positive, respectful workplace culture. When this broader view of success is promoted, it can foster an environment where attraction is based on genuine respect and admiration for a diverse range of qualities and accomplishments.

To sum up, the interplay of success and attraction within the context of Erotism in Management is a nuanced phenomenon, akin to a carefully choreographed dance. It demands conscious awareness, understanding, and careful navigation from everyone involved.

Unleashing the Power: Erotism as an Unexplored Business Resource

As our understanding of effective business practices evolves, so does our appreciation for the complex interplay of human dynamics within the professional world. The rapidly changing landscape of modern workplaces continually demands new perspectives and approaches. It is in this context that the potential of erotism as a largely unexplored business resource comes to the fore.

Erotism, a concept often confined to the realm of personal and intimate relationships, refers to the acknowledgment and expression of human desires, passions, and emotions. Far from its typical association with explicit sexuality or indecency, erotism in the professional world encapsulates a spectrum of deeply human aspects that play a significant role in shaping interpersonal dynamics, decision-making processes, and overall workplace culture.

Incorporating erotism into business management requires a nuanced understanding of its applications and implications. It is not about turning the professional setting into a space for inappropriate conduct or creating an uncomfortable atmosphere. Instead, it is about tapping into the rich wellspring of human emotions and desires that often remain underexplored in conventional business practices.

The journey to unleashing the power of erotism in the business world begins with recognizing its importance and understanding its potential impacts. The conventional business environment, with its emphasis on logic, rationality, and results, often relegates human emotions and desires to the background. However, successful organizations are those that can effectively manage and leverage the full spectrum of human elements, including those encapsulated by the concept of erotism.

There are several key facets to consider when discussing the potential of erotism as an unexplored business resource. These include its influence on communication, collaboration, creativity, leadership, and organizational culture.

In terms of communication, the concept of erotism can revolutionize the way employees interact within the workplace. Communication is not merely the exchange of information; it is the conduit through which human emotions, desires, and passions are expressed. Recognizing and incorporating these elements into workplace communication can lead to more authentic, engaging, and effective exchanges.

An environment where employees feel comfortable expressing their feelings and desires will foster open, honest, and meaningful dialogues.

From a collaboration standpoint, erotism has the potential to transform the dynamics within teams and across departments. By acknowledging and celebrating the diverse range of human desires and emotions, organizations can foster an environment of mutual trust and respect. This environment is conducive to collaboration and encourages individuals to bring their unique perspectives and ideas to the table.

In the realm of creativity, acknowledging the sensual and passionate sides of individuals can unlock their innovative potential. When employees are encouraged to tap into their deepest desires and emotions, they are more likely to think outside the box and come up with groundbreaking ideas. Erotism in business management serves as a catalyst that can inspire individuals to challenge the status quo and explore new possibilities.

When it comes to leadership, the power of erotism can redefine the traditional notions of authority and influence. Instead of relying solely on hierarchical power structures, leaders who incorporate erotism into their management style acknowledge the importance of emotional intelligence, empathy, and genuine human connection.

By cultivating an atmosphere of mutual respect and trust, leaders can inspire their teams to reach their fullest potential.

In terms of organizational culture, the integration of erotism can transform the workplace into a more engaging, fulfilling, and dynamic environment. An organizational culture that values and celebrates the sensual, passionate, and deeply human aspects of its employees fosters a sense of belonging, enhances job satisfaction, and improves employee retention.

However, it is important to note that incorporating erotism into business management is not without its challenges. The concept of erotism can be subjective and vary significantly across different cultures, societies, and individual comfort levels. Therefore, organizations must be cautious in their approach and ensure that the incorporation of erotism respects diversity and individual boundaries.

It is also crucial to maintain a clear distinction between professional and personal boundaries to avoid any potential misuse of power or inappropriate conduct. Managers and leaders should establish clear guidelines and ethical standards to ensure that the expression of erotism within the workplace is respectful, consensual, and aligned with the organization's values.

The potential of erotism as an unexplored business resource is vast, and the journey to unleashing its power can be transformative for both individuals and organizations. By challenging conventional business practices and embracing the deeply human aspects of employees, organizations can create a more vibrant, dynamic, and fulfilling work environment.

The integration of erotism into business management paves the way for innovative practices that can revolutionize the way organizations operate. It fosters a culture of authenticity, trust, and respect where individuals feel valued, engaged, and motivated. Ultimately, the exploration and incorporation of erotism in the business environment can lead to the growth and success of an organization.

Looking ahead, it is also crucial to consider how the concept of erotism can be leveraged to attract and retain top talent in the increasingly competitive global market. The notion of a workplace that respects, celebrates, and harnesses the spectrum of human desires, passions, and emotions can be a strong draw for potential employees, particularly in the younger generation that places high value on personal fulfillment, authenticity, and creative freedom.

When organizations demonstrate a commitment to nurturing a holistic, sensual, and emotionally connected work environment, they create a unique employer brand that sets them apart.

Moreover, the use of erotism as a business resource can provide a new lens through which to understand and manage diversity within the workplace. In an era marked by the rapid globalization of business, workplaces are becoming more diverse than ever before. With this diversity comes a wide range of passions, desires, and ways of expressing them. By utilizing erotism as a tool, managers can create an inclusive environment where these varied expressions are valued and leveraged for the benefit of the organization.

Further, the transformative potential of erotism extends beyond the internal environment of an organization. When an organization radiates authenticity, passion, and sensual engagement, it can also have a significant impact on the perception of external stakeholders such as clients, customers, partners, and even competitors.

Such organizations may be perceived as more innovative, vibrant, and forward-thinking, potentially leading to enhanced business relationships, increased customer loyalty, and improved market standing.

In the long run, the integration of erotism can play a role in redefining the very nature of success in the business world. Traditionally, success has been predominantly defined in terms of financial metrics and market share.

However, as erotism takes root within organizations and starts reshaping their culture and practices, it opens up the possibility of broadening this definition of success.

Success can start to encompass not just financial prosperity, but also the well-being of employees, the quality of interpersonal relationships, the level of creative freedom, and the cultivation of an authentic, emotionally connected work environment.

It's essential to emphasize that the utilization of erotism as a business resource is not a one-size-fits-all approach. The way in which it is implemented may look different from one organization to another, and even from one team to another within the same organization.

Each implementation needs to be carefully tailored to the specific needs, values, and culture of the organization.

Finally, while the journey to unleashing the power of erotism in the business world can be transformative, it is by no means a straightforward one. It requires continuous learning, adaptation, and courage to challenge traditional norms and paradigms.

It necessitates a deep understanding of human emotions, desires, and passions, and a commitment to respect and celebrate them.

With these considerations at the forefront, the journey can lead organizations to new heights of innovation, fulfillment, and success.

In conclusion, erotism, as an unexplored business resource, holds tremendous potential for transforming the business landscape. It is an opportunity to enrich work experience, cultivate stronger relationships, inspire innovation, and enhance the effectiveness of leadership.

Despite the potential challenges and sensitivities surrounding its incorporation, with careful and respectful implementation, erotism can indeed be a powerful asset in the world of business management.

So, what is SENSUAL INTELLIGENCE?

Sensual Intelligence, especially in a business and management context, is the ability to effectively perceive, understand, and utilize nonverbal cues such as tone, body language, and emotional energy to enhance interpersonal connections, drive motivation, and lead teams more effectively.

It involves tapping into one's senses to gather nuanced information about one's environment, fostering a more profound understanding of people's motivations, attitudes, and responses.

Sensual Intelligence is the art of harnessing the power of the senses to cultivate a captivating leadership style. It is about resonating with others on a deep, intuitive level, transcending the realm of verbal communication.

Sensual Intelligence is the invisible thread that weaves an immersive tapestry of motivation, engagement, and loyalty among team members.

In the corporate world, Sensual Intelligence is a tool for fostering meaningful relationships, enabling leaders to attune to their team's subtle emotional cues. It is about creating an environment that appeals to the senses, making workplaces more engaging, productive, and harmonious. It's about leading not just with the mind, but also with the heart and soul.

Sensual Intelligence allows a leader to create a stimulating atmosphere, an environment that not only appeals to the intellect but also touches the heart. It unlocks a leader's ability to inspire creativity, kindle passion, and instigate innovation.

This form of intelligence fosters a deep understanding of the team's motivations, enabling the leader to align the team's passions and talents with organizational goals.

Leaders who master Sensual Intelligence can transform their leadership style from being merely directive to becoming genuinely inspirational.

They become adept at using non-verbal cues, emotional energy, and personal charisma to influence and guide their teams, resulting in a workforce that's more motivated, engaged, and productive.

Sensual Intelligence extends beyond the confines of office walls and business hours. It is a comprehensive way of engaging with the world around us. It's the fine-tuning of senses to the subtle shifts in our surroundings, an enriched understanding of how our environment affects us, and in turn, how we affect others.

This form of intelligence imparts a unique advantage to leaders: the ability to shape the corporate atmosphere. Sensual Intelligence brings aesthetics, ambiance, and personal interaction into play, making them integral elements of a team's dynamics.

It goes beyond the conventional to include an appreciation for the aesthetics of a workplace, understanding the impact of a pleasing, comfortable environment on productivity and creativity.

As leaders, leveraging Sensual Intelligence means engaging with your team on a deeper level, going beyond words and actions to include the realm of emotions and senses.

It's about being attuned to the emotional climate of the team and proactively shaping it to foster a positive, encouraging, and inspiring work environment.

This includes everything from the physical comfort of the workplace to the emotional tone of interactions, recognizing that all of these elements combined play a pivotal role in employee satisfaction, motivation, and productivity.

Leaders with high Sensual Intelligence are empathetic and emotionally connected, not just intellectually competent.

They understand the emotional needs of their teams and take steps to address them. They can read between the lines, picking up on unspoken feelings and subtle cues that others might miss.

They are attuned to the emotional undercurrents within their teams and are adept at navigating these complexities to maintain a positive and productive atmosphere.

Furthermore, Sensual Intelligence promotes an open, receptive attitude towards feedback. Leaders with a high level of Sensual Intelligence not only communicate effectively but also listen keenly, making their team members feel valued and understood. They are more approachable, fostering a culture of transparency and trust.

Sensual Intelligence in a leader is like a magnet, drawing in talent and dedication, fostering loyalty and collaboration, and building a team that is motivated, committed, and highly effective. It is the secret ingredient that turns a good leader into a great one, and a productive team into an extraordinary one.

In essence, Sensual Intelligence is not just about how you interact with the world; it's about how you perceive, interpret, and influence it. It's about leading with empathy, integrity, and a deep understanding of the emotional landscape of your team. It's an indispensable tool for any leader who aims not just to manage but to inspire, motivate, and lead with distinction.

Leaders who are able to understand, decode, and utilize their sensual intelligence within their workplace can create more inclusive and harmonious environments. These leaders promote a culture of understanding, where every team member's emotion and experience are acknowledged, respected, and valued.

This is not a trivial matter - studies have shown that workplaces with a high level of emotional intelligence tend to have lower turnover rates, higher levels of employee satisfaction, and increased productivity.

Sensual intelligence also encourages leaders to remain present, fostering an atmosphere of mindfulness within the workplace. This state of being present is not just beneficial to the individual, but also to the team as a whole. It promotes a culture of attentiveness, where all team members feel heard and understood. This state of mindfulness also allows leaders to respond rather than react to situations, resulting in well-thought-out decisions that are aligned with the team's best interests.

Moreover, leaders with a high level of sensual intelligence are often more adaptable. They are keenly attuned to the subtle changes within their environment and can swiftly respond and adapt to these shifts.

This adaptability is a key asset in today's fast-paced and ever-evolving business landscape. It allows these leaders to stay one step ahead, preparing their teams for changes before they happen and guiding them smoothly through periods of transition.

Sensual intelligence can also contribute to leaders' personal growth. By tuning into their senses and emotions, these leaders develop a deeper understanding of themselves - their motivations, their strengths, their weaknesses.

This self-awareness is a vital trait for effective leadership. It allows these leaders to identify areas for improvement, work towards personal growth, and inspire their team members to do the same.

Leaders with sensual intelligence also foster a more innovative environment. By tapping into their senses, they can inspire creativity and original thinking within their teams. They encourage their team members to approach problems from different perspectives, resulting in innovative solutions that would not have been discovered through traditional problem-solving methods.

Furthermore, sensual intelligence allows leaders to connect with their teams on a human level. They are able to empathize with their team members' emotions and experiences, building strong bonds based on trust and mutual respect. This emotional connection can enhance team cohesion, promote collaboration, and ultimately lead to a more engaged and committed workforce.

In conclusion, sensual intelligence is a powerful tool for leaders in the modern workplace. It fosters a culture of empathy, mindfulness, adaptability, self-awareness, and innovation. Leaders who master this form of intelligence can transform their teams and organizations, driving not only productivity and efficiency but also job satisfaction, personal growth, and team cohesion. As the business landscape continues to evolve, the role of sensual intelligence in leadership will only become more critical. Thus, it is essential for leaders to develop this form of intelligence and integrate it into their leadership style.

How can we measure sensual intelligence?

Measuring sensual intelligence indeed poses a unique challenge due to its multifaceted and somewhat elusive nature. Nevertheless, it's possible to assess this form of intelligence by focusing on several key areas and developing a composite score based on multiple indicators.

One of the primary aspects to consider in measuring sensual intelligence is the individual's ability to perceive and understand non-verbal cues.

This can include reading body language, picking up on changes in tone, and discerning emotional undercurrents from facial expressions or other subtle signs.

These abilities can be evaluated through simulations or role-playing exercises where individuals have to interpret non-verbal cues and respond accordingly. Their performance in these exercises can provide a valuable indicator of their sensual intelligence.

Another important aspect to assess is an individual's level of empathy. Empathy is a key component of sensual intelligence, allowing one to understand and share the feelings of others.

This can be gauged through personal interviews, psychological assessments, or 360-degree feedback from colleagues and subordinates. Questions or scenarios designed to understand how an individual responds to the emotions of others, or how well they are able to put themselves in others' shoes, can help measure this aspect.

A person's awareness and responsiveness to their environment also forms an integral part of sensual intelligence. This includes their sensitivity to aesthetics, their ability to create a pleasing and engaging atmosphere, and their understanding of how different environments affect people's moods and productivity.

This could be assessed through direct observation, feedback from team members, or even by assessing the individual's workspace or their approach to organizing events and meetings.

The ability to adapt to changes and respond effectively to new situations is another key facet of sensual intelligence. This adaptability can be measured through specific tasks or challenges that require individuals to adjust their strategies or approaches in response to shifting circumstances.

Lastly, an individual's ability to communicate effectively and connect with others on a deep, emotional level is a vital aspect of sensual intelligence. This can be evaluated through feedback from peers and subordinates, assessment of their ability to motivate and inspire others, and observation of their communication style and effectiveness in team settings.

Once these different aspects are assessed, the results can be normalized to a common scale to allow for comparison. By combining these normalized scores, a comprehensive sensual intelligence KPI can be developed. This can provide a valuable tool for identifying areas of strength and potential areas for improvement, aiding in personal development, team formation, and leadership selection.

However, it's crucial to remember that sensual intelligence, like other forms of intelligence, is not static but can be developed and enhanced over time. Regular reassessment and feedback can help individuals improve their sensual intelligence, leading to more effective leadership, better team dynamics, and improved performance.

Therefore, while the measurement of sensual intelligence can be complex, with the right approach, it can provide valuable insights into an individual's capabilities and potential. The key lies in recognizing the multifaceted nature of this form of intelligence and using a comprehensive and holistic approach to its assessment.

Here's a suggested process:

Standardize Scores: First, you'll need to ensure all measures are standardized, meaning they are on the same scale. If one measure uses a scale of 1-5, and another uses a scale of 1-10, you'll need to convert the scores to a common scale, such as 0-100%.

Weight Scores: Depending on the importance of each measure in the context of Sensual Intelligence, assign a weight to each KPI. This is important because some measures might be more directly related to Sensual Intelligence than others. For instance, you might decide Emotional Intelligence Scores carry a weight of 0.3 (30%), Employee Engagement 0.25 (25%), Communication Effectiveness 0.2 (20%), Workplace Environment Ratings 0.15 (15%), and Employee Turnover Rate 0.1 (10%). Ensure that all the weights add up to 1 (or 100%).

Calculate Composite Score: Multiply the standardized score for each measure by its respective weight. Then, sum all these weighted scores to get the composite score. This composite score is your Sensual Intelligence KPI.

For example, let's say we have the following scores for an individual:

- Emotional Intelligence Scores: 75 out of 100
- Employee Engagement: 80 out of 100
- Communication Effectiveness: 85 out of 100
- Workplace Environment Ratings: 90 out of 100
- Employee Turnover Rate: 10 out of 100 (for rates like turnover, lower is better, so you might want to invert this score to fit the scale, i.e., 100 - original score, giving us a score of 90 out of 100 for this example)

Using the weights from earlier, the composite score would be:

(75 * 0.3) + (80 * 0.25) + (85 * 0.2) + (90 * 0.15) + (90 * 0.1) = **82.5**

This composite score (82.5) serves as a Sensual Intelligence KPI. It summarizes the individual's Sensual Intelligence as a single number.

What does the SENSUAL INTELLIGENCE KPI tell you?

Sensual Intelligence KPI of 82.5 out of 100 suggests that the individual has a strong ability to leverage their understanding of emotions, non-verbal cues, and human connection in a professional context.

This score indicates that the individual is likely effective at creating an engaging and positive work environment, and they're likely to be skilled at using empathy and emotional understanding to facilitate stronger team relationships.

Here's a breakdown based on the components of the score:

- *Emotional Intelligence Scores*: With a score of 75 out of 100, the individual shows good emotional understanding and management. They're likely to be self-aware, able to manage their emotions, understand others' emotions, and use this understanding to navigate interpersonal relationships effectively.

- *Employee Engagement*: Scoring 80 indicates that the individual is successful at engaging their team members. They likely use their emotional and sensual intelligence to create an environment where employees feel valued, involved, and committed to their work.

- *Communication Effectiveness*: A score of 85 shows strong skills in communication. The individual can likely articulate their thoughts clearly and is adept at using non-verbal cues. They understand the importance of tone, body language, and timing in effective communication.

- *Workplace Environment Ratings*: Scoring 90 suggests that the individual excels at creating a positive and motivating work environment. They likely understand the emotional and sensual elements that contribute to a comfortable and productive workplace.

- *Employee Turnover Rate*: A score of 90 (after inversion) suggests that the individual is able to retain talent effectively, indicative of a positive work environment and strong team relationships.

The Sensual Intelligence KPI, with a composite score of 82.5 out of 100, is indicative of an individual's profound ability to utilize and integrate their understanding of emotions, sensory cues, and interpersonal connections within a professional setting.

On a macro level, a high score such as 82.5 is indicative of an individual's significant strength in harnessing and channeling emotional and sensory acumen for creating productive and positive work environments.

This score suggests that this individual isn't just cognizant of the hard skills and traditional metrics of performance but is also attuned to the nuanced aspects of human interactions and the psychological subtleties that govern a workspace.

To put it in simpler terms, an individual with a high score is likely to be a people's person who uses their emotional and sensory knowledge to understand their team members on a deeper level and connect with them more effectively.

They value human connection and are skilled at fostering it, which can greatly enhance team cohesiveness and productivity.

The Sensual Intelligence KPI also suggests that the individual is skilled at leveraging emotional intelligence and non-verbal communication to influence, guide, and inspire their team. It indicates a mastery in creating an engaging and uplifting workplace atmosphere that not only appeals to the intellect but also touches the heart.

Furthermore, the high KPI implies that the individual is adept at aligning their team's passions and talents with organizational goals by gaining a deep understanding of their team's motivations. They can motivate their team members to become more engaged, committed, and productive.

A high score in Sensual Intelligence also suggests that the individual may have a knack for decreasing employee turnover. They are likely capable of creating a workplace environment that employees find satisfying and rewarding, which encourages them to remain with the organization.

Lastly, this composite score suggests that the individual values feedback, likely fostering a culture of transparency and trust.

Their communication style not only effectively conveys their thoughts but also invites others to share their perspectives, making their team members feel heard and valued.

In summary, a high Sensual Intelligence KPI score of 82.5 signifies an individual's exceptional ability to leverage emotional understanding and sensory perceptions to enhance team dynamics, improve communication, and foster a positive and engaging workplace environment.

Their strengths likely lie in empathetic leadership, effective communication, and the creation of an inclusive, supportive, and motivating atmosphere, ultimately driving employee engagement, productivity, and retention.

Afterword from the Author: The Power to Transform

The closing of one chapter is always the opening of another, and as we conclude this exploration of sensuality in leadership, it is my deepest hope that a new journey is just beginning for you. The journey that leads to transformation. To growth. To a radical reimagining of leadership as we know it.

Throughout this book, we have dared to venture off the beaten path, into the mysterious and exciting realm of erotism in management. We have lifted the veil on what has often been considered a taboo, unveiling the profound power of sensuality, seduction, and personal magnetism as tools for effective leadership.

We have opened our minds and hearts to the notion of viewing our employees not merely as parts of a well-oiled machine but as complex, sentient beings with a diverse range of desires and motivations.

We have come to understand that being an effective leader is about so much more than simply managing resources and executing strategies. It's about connecting. Engaging. Inspiring.

Our exploration has led us to the concept of Sensual Intelligence, a term that embodies the seamless blend of emotional connection, personal magnetism, and the judicious use of seduction in leadership.

We've learned that, when harnessed effectively, this kind of intelligence can not only transform our leadership style but can also revolutionize our workplaces, turning them into spaces of vibrancy, motivation, and engagement.

As we draw to a close, I am confident that the seeds we have sown within these pages have the potential to grow into powerful instruments of change. I hope that you will carry these insights into your work, your relationships, and your leadership practice. I hope you feel inspired to break free from the traditional confines of leadership and dare to lead with seduction, sensuality, and a deep emotional connection.

This book has been far more than a collection of concepts and theories. It has been a call to action, a beacon guiding you towards a transformative shift in your perspective on leadership. It is my hope that as you turn the final pages, you are not ending a journey, but beginning a new one filled with growth, engagement, and profound transformation.

I implore you to reflect upon these principles, to put them into practice in your interactions with your teams and colleagues.

Share these insights, instigate conversations, stimulate debates. This is the kind of book that sparks dialogues, invigorates team meetings, and provokes introspection during solitary moments of reflection.

I am deeply grateful for your companionship on this journey and for your willingness to embrace an unconventional perspective.

As you step forward, carrying with you these fresh insights, I trust that you will experience the transformative power of sensual intelligence and that you will, in turn, inspire transformation in others.

The power to transform lies within you. It is my greatest hope that this book has offered you a key to unlock that power.

As you move forward, I urge you to let the principles of seduction, sensuality, and deep human connection guide you as you redefine your leadership narrative.

The future of leadership beckons—a future that is vibrant, powerful, engaging, and profoundly human. A future that is not just managed, but truly led. And I am excited to see you, dear reader, leading the way.

With deep appreciation,

Antonio Garrido

THE END

Manufactured by Amazon.ca
Acheson, AB

13343875R00186